EXETER CITY

A FILE OF FASCINATING FOOTBALL FACTS

MIKE BLACKSTONE

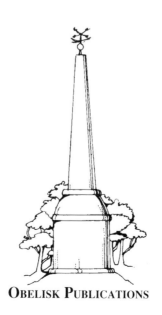

OBELISK PUBLICATIONS

ALSO IN THIS SERIES:
Torquay United–the First 70 Years by Laura Joint

ABOUT THE AUTHOR:
Exmouth-born Mike Blackstone has followed the exploits of Exeter City since attending his first match at St James's Park in 1959. Together with his father, he quickly became interested in collecting statistics on the club. They now possess probably the most comprehensive history anywhere concerning Exeter city Football club, since its formation in 1904. Mike has contributed many football related articles to various newspapers and publications, as well as editing the award-winning Exmouth Town Football Club match programme for an eight year period.

ACKNOWLEDGEMENTS:
Jim Blackstone for collecting Exeter City statistics and stories with me, and for proof reading the manuscript. The photographs have been begged and borrowed from a number of sources and I would particularly like to thank the following for their help, skill and co-operation: Dave Fisher, Tony Ellis, Pat Wakeham, Ian Jubb, Chips Barber and the Express and Echo.

OTHER BOOKS ABOUT EXETER FROM OBELISK PUBLICATIONS:
The Lost City of Exeter, Chips Barber
An Exeter Boyhood, Frank Retter
The Great Little Exeter Book, Chips Barber
Exeter in Colour, Chips Barber
The Ghosts of Exeter, Sally and Chips Barber
Talking About Topsham, Sara Vernon
An Alphington Album, P. Aplin & J. Gaskell

For further details about these or any of our other titles about Devon, please contact us at 2 Church Hill, Pinhoe, Exeter EX4 9ER, Tel: 0392 68556

First published in 1992 by
Obelisk Publications,
2 Church Hill, Pinhoe, Exeter, Devon
Designed by Chips and Sally Barber
Typeset by Sally Barber
Printed in Great Britain by
Penwell Print Ltd, Callington, Cornwall

All Rights Reserved
© Mike Blackstone 1992

INTRODUCTION

Long before the days of yellow and red cards, there was a sending off which made front page headlines – "ICE CREAM SALES LADY SENT OFF". A match at St James's Park, in the mid 1960s, was halted because the referee was distracted by the said lady and promptly gave her her marching orders! It was unusual episodes like this which prompted the compilation of this book; stories which would normally be lost in the mists of time. Through the years all manner of strange and silly stories have arisen in connection with Exeter City so this is not a book of statistics – although from time to time they crop up – it portrays the human side of Exeter City. It is a much-loved football club which has enjoyed or endured its share of frustrations, follies and foibles. To that end I have dipped into the club's past to reveal some of its many faces. Covered are such diverse subjects as take-over bids, problems with pork pies and failing floodlights. The ground itself occupies some of the limelight with aspects such as ground safety considered.

Exeter City is a homely 'little' club, a true supporters club, and St James's Park is an intimate ground. It may be a million miles from the likes of the Liverpools and Manchester Uniteds of this world but the great majority of fans wouldn't trade places with their more illustrious Football League bedfellows. There is a very special quality about following Exeter City, a unique sense of belonging. It is a struggle for a club like Exeter City to survive and it is my fervent hope that they continue to battle on against all the odds which they may face.

Here, then, is a File of Fascinating Football Facts about Exeter City. I hope you will enjoy this potted look at events which span four 'score' years and more – long may it all continue.

ABANDONED GAMES

Exeter City have been involved in several abandoned matches, with at least three having occurred during FA Cup ties. The first happened on 23rd November 1910 in a home tie against Reading. The match had been switched to the County Ground in Exeter, because the St James's Park pitch was not big enough to meet FA regulations. With the score standing at 1-1, fog caused the abandonment in the 80th minute. Exeter won 1-0 in the re-arranged match back at the County Ground five days later.

City were losing 5-0 at Southampton in the first round in January 1925 when the match fell foul of fog again in the seventy seventh minute. City lost the re-arranged game 3-1.

In December 1936 Exeter's match at non-leaguers Walthamstow Avenue came to a premature end after sixty five minutes with the scoreline standing at 1-1 due to the ever thickening fog which enveloped the ground. The match attendance of 11,131 was a record for the London club. The re-arranged game five days later ended with City winning 3-2 in front of 8,000 spectators.

A few Football League fixtures have also been abandoned for various reasons. On two occasions matches were stopped abruptly because of bad light. The first time was in November 1919 when Exeter were drawing 0-0 at Crystal Palace. With just five minutes remaining the match was abandoned as it became impossible to follow the play. The Palace crowd were none too happy with the decision and the referee, Mr Rundle, was jostled as he left the field. Connor of Crystal Palace and City goalkeeper Dick Pym protected the referee from any further violence.

The second match to be abandoned through bad light was on 23rd November 1946, again in London, this time at Leyton Orient. The match had run for eighty one minutes before being halted with Orient leading 2-1.

The City Reserves were involved in an abandoned Western League game at St James's Park on Boxing Day 1963. Their opponents, Bristol City Reserves, were leading 4-1 when in the seventieth minute the referee abandoned the game after the foggy conditions progressively got worse and worse.

Fog was the cause of another abandonment in March 1972, this time at Grimsby Town. City's Fourth Division fixture was abandoned after just eighteen minutes with the fog swirling in off the sea. The referee halted the game for ten minutes to see if the conditions would improve, but with visibility down to twenty five yards he had no alternative but to call a halt with the scoreline goalless.

The only Football League match to be abandoned at St James's Park was on 6th April 1991 against Shrewsbury Town, with Exeter 1-0 ahead, when proceedings were brought to a halt because of a waterlogged pitch. There were puddles all over the playing surface so the referee, after a half-time inspection, called the game off.

One of the most unusual abandoned games involved the Exeter City Reserves side at Plymouth Argyle in a Plymouth and District League match in December 1919. The rain fell throughout the first half making conditions virtually impossible. However, they suited Argyle for they led 6-0 at half-time. During the interval four of City's players refused to return for the second half because of the conditions, so the game

Keith Harvey in the early 1970s, baling water at St James's Park

restarted with Exeter taking to the field with just seven players! Plymouth added three more goals before the referee abandoned the proceedings midway through the half with the heavy rain still falling. The Plymouth and District League ordered the result to stand.

Exeter City's Fourth Division match at Aldershot in December 1976 was abandoned with just three minutes of the game remaining when the floodlights failed. City were trailing 1-0 at the time. The Football League refused to allow the result to stand and ordered the game to be replayed. In the rearranged match luck was again on Exeter's side, for with just seconds remaining, full back John Templeman scored a vital equaliser to make the final score 2-2.

ARRESTED

Four Sunderland players were arrested at the Salston Hotel, Ottery St Mary in November 1989. This followed an incident in Exeter's city centre the previous evening, after Sunderland had drawn 2-2 in a Football League Cup tie at St James's Park. The players involved were goalkeeper Tim Carter, Gordon Armstrong one of the Sunderland goalscorers against the City, and Sunderland's two substitutes, John Kay and Paul Williams. All four players were later released by the police with no further action taken against Carter and Armstrong.

ATTENDANCES

What happened to the missing thirty one spectators? Whilst the official attendance for Exeter City's FA Cup quarter final replay at St James's Park in 1931 is shown in all the record books as being 20,984 – a club record – the actual attendance given in the *Express and Echo* newspaper report of the game was 21,015!

King's Lynn set an attendance record of 12,500 at their ground, when they

played Exeter City in an FA Cup first round tie in 1951. City won the game 3-1.

Stockport County recorded their then lowest ever attendance (1,335) for the visit of Exeter City on 24th November 1984, and promptly blamed the City for their insistence that the game went ahead on a Saturday afternoon rather than a Friday night. Exeter had refused Stockport's request to play a Friday match at Edgley Park and consequently the attendance suffered.

Only 693 spectators were present at Borough Park for Workington's home fixture in the Fourth Division with Exeter City in December 1973. Workington won 3-1 with Exeter fielding debutants Keith Bowker and Peter Hatch who had been signed from Birmingham City and Oxford United respectively.

Average Football League attendances at St James's Park showed an alarming drop of nearly 38 per cent between the 1961/62 and 1971/72 seasons. Not surprisingly they peaked in 1963/64 when Exeter City won promotion to the Third Division. The season by season averages were as follows: 1961/62 – 6,211; 1962/63 – 5,958; 1963/64 – 7,296; 1964/65 – 6,459; 1965/66 – 4,500; 1966/67 – 3,990; 1967/68 – 3,886; 1968/69 – 5,084; 1969/70 – 4,918; 1970/71 – 4,687; 1971/72 – 3,857 .

As a comparison when City again won promotion to Division Three in 1989/90, the average home attendance was 4,859.

BASKETBALL

Exeter City applied to join the local Basketball League in 1965 following an idea from club secretary Dick Miller, who was a keen player himself. Ten players expressed an interest in playing for the City Basketball team, namely

Des Anderson, Peter Arbury, Mike Balson, Alan Barnett, Wilf Carter, Bobby House, Les MacDonald, Phil Richardson, Cecil Smyth and Chris Taylor.

BOMB SCARE

Nothing moves a football crowd, not even a bomb scare! The game at Rotherham United against Exeter City in November 1974 was just about to kick-off when a police announcement was made over the public address system. They had received an anonymous telephone call that a bomb had been planted at the Millmoor ground and was timed to explode at 3.25 p.m. The gates were opened for anyone who wanted to leave, but no one appeared to do so! The appointed time passed without incident, and the game ended in a 1-1 draw in front of 4,623 unharmed, and certainly unconcerned, spectators.

BOWLING ALLEY

In August 1961 the Football Club submitted plans to the Exeter City Council to build a £150,000 bowling alley complex in partnership with a developer. This could have been sited behind the Big Bank end of the ground where a two storey building, consisting of ten bowling lanes on each floor was to be constructed, together with an indoor gymnasium which could have been used by the City players for training purposes. Improved access to the ground from Old Tiverton Road were also part of the plans. A car park with thirty spaces would be constructed, and the house which the Football Club owned – number 18 Old Tiverton Road – was to be demolished. The City Council rejected the scheme because the area was regarded as being a residential one and would seriously affect the neighbouring properties. Exeter City then appealed against the decision, a public enquiry being held in May 1962. Nearby residents presented a petition against the plans; they were concerned that their properties would be devalued, and because of the vastly increased noise level that was expected. After a site inspection the development was refused.

BREAK-INS

Twenty seven bottles of lemonade and ginger beer were among items stolen from the refreshment hut at St James's Park in August 1949. Empty bottles were left strewn over the pitch. Billiard balls were stolen from the players' recreation hut on the popular side of the ground and a number of cues were thrown about the floor. The intruders also forced their way into the boardroom and drank bottles of port, sherry, and whisky before leaving – no doubt in good spirits! This was the fourth break-in that Exeter City had suffered in eight months and by far the most serious as locks were also forced and broken on cupboards containing playing kit and other gear.

There was another break-in during January 1961. Vandals wrecked and uprooted one set of goal posts at the Big Bank end of the ground and ripped open the nets.

The team of 1970/71 features the two City players who chased a thief. Standing left to right: Keith Harvey (trainer), John Wingate, Brian Sharples, Jimmy Blain, Peter Shearing, Mike Balson, Bob Wilson, Graham Parker, Joe Gadston, John Newman (manager). Seated (L to R) John Corr, Campbell Crawford, Alan Banks, Barry Rowan, John Mitten, John Giles, Steve Morris, Fred Binney.

An odd sight greeted Exeter City officials when they arrived at St James's Park in August 1966, but they were far from amused. The collection trays from the fruit machines were found placed on the penalty spots on the pitch, and a change machine was hanging from a goal net. The fruit machines, which were kept in a corridor beneath the Grandstand, had been broken into, and approximately £30 cash was taken.

The club offices were broken into in February 1968. Despite the security alarms being set off by the intruders, there was still time to ransack the premises, but nothing was stolen.

A thief was caught in January 1971 by City players Steve Morris and John Corr, who were both training at St Luke's College. They had noticed a man running away from the changing rooms. The two players gave chase and caught him. It was later discovered that he had been through the players' clothes in the changing rooms stealing money and keys.

The boardroom was broken into in October 1973, where bottles of spirits were removed. The cheeky thief drank a 'tot' before he left, leaving behind an empty glass!

BUY-A-PLAYER

Exeter City launched a 'Buy-A-Player' scheme in March 1972. A target of £5,000 was set to be raised in three months, so that a player or players could be bought to strengthen the squad in time for the following season. Commercial manager John Hillier launched the scheme saying he was confident that sufficient money would be raised to go towards buying a player. One of the first events organised to raise money was a sponsored walk by City supporter Peter Hawkins of Axminster, who walked from his home to a game at St James's Park raising £25. A 'Golden Admission Gate' was opened at one of the turnstiles at the St James's Road end of the ground, whereby supporters were invited to pay 50p instead of the more usual 30p to stand on the terraces.

CHARABANCS

The Exeter City team undertook what turned out to be an arduous journey to Merthyr Town for their Third Division South fixture on Good Friday 1922. The party had left Exeter the day before the match by charabanc and stopped overnight at a Cardiff hotel.

On the day of the game however, and en route to Merthyr, the charabanc broke down. With time fast approaching kick-off, several cars were requisitioned to enable the team to reach the ground. Despite their ill prepared arrival, City did manage to hold Merthyr to a goalless draw.

The charabanc was repaired in time for Exeter's return to Devon straight after the match, the party arriving back in Devon at 3.30 a.m. on the Sunday morning.

CHRISTMAS DAY

The first professional match to be played at St James's Park on a Christmas Day took place in 1908. An attendance of 11,500 saw Exeter City defeat Millwall 2-1, with James 'Daisy' Bell, and Andy McGuigan scoring the goals.

Happy Christmas Exeter City! That was certainly the case on Christmas Day 1946, as they travelled to Brighton and Hove Albion for a Third Division South fixture and duly won 6-1 with Bill Owen scoring a hat-trick in front of an attendance of 7,777.

The first Exeter City Christmas Day fixture to be played at St James's Park after the Second World War took place in 1948. The visitors were Brighton and Hove Albion for a Third Division South encounter. It was expected that the attendance would suffer as there were no buses running, however many of the 'country supporters' were catered for with additional trains stopping at St James's Park Halt. Seven thousand spectators made it to the game which ended all square at 1-1, Angus Mackay scoring the Exeter goal.

Half back Ivan Armes has the distinction of making his Exeter City first team debut on Christmas Day 1951. Having been signed from Norwich City three days earlier, Ivan made a successful debut, which included scoring the third Exeter goal at St James's Park in a 4-0 victory over rivals Torquay United.

The last Football League match to be played at St James's Park on a Christmas Day was in 1954, when Swindon Town were the visitors. City won 2-1 with goals from Eddie Murphy and Ray John before an attendance of 6,527.

The City Reserves team had the distinction of playing the last ever Christmas Day fixture at the Park in 1957. Goals from Ted Calland and Dilwyn Hill gave them a 2-0 win over Weymouth in a Southern League match.

The last Christmas Day fixture that the first team played was also in 1957, at Torquay United. Peter Rapley, Arnold Mitchell and Johnny Nicholls scored for the City, with Ernie Pym replying for Torquay in front of an attendance of 6,774.

CLUBCALL

In line with many other clubs, Exeter City launched their own Clubcall telephone line in August 1988. Daily updates of all the latest news from the club, together with interviews, could be heard by dialling 0898 121634. The first month of the service attracted 950 calls, whilst in the following month a further 1,812 calls were made.

CLUB SONG

An official club song, 'The Exeter City March', was released in November 1971. It was played to a 'captive audience' prior to the home match with Brentford at St James's Park. Like so many football songs, it was never going to become a number one chart success. In fact it was pretty certain that it would not have reached 1,001 in the charts!

Nevertheless, the Exeter City squad recorded yet another couple of songs during the summer of 1972. A record was released with the 'A' side featuring the players singing the blandly named, 'Swing Along With City', and striker Fred Binney, a former member of a Plymouth pop group, performing solo on the flip side with another equally 'memorable' little ditty entitled 'Football Fan'.

COMEDIANS

Whilst it may be true to say several 'comedians' have worn the red and white of Exeter City in its long history, the club really were graced with a famous one in October 1971! The late Eric Morecombe who was appearing at the ABC Cinema in Exeter with his partner-in-laughs, Ernie Wise, popped into St James's Park for City's match with Southport. He was invited into the dressing room to meet the players, and kept them amused in his usual, and much missed style. And what had happened to 'little Ern'? He decided to visit Sidmouth for the day. Perhaps he knew something that Eric and the 3,408, supporters present at the game didn't – for Exeter City lost 3-1.

Eric Morecombe was not the only comedian to meet the City players. For back in July 1967, the Exeter players visited Torquay as part of their pre-season training programme (they played golf and also went swimming!). In

Exeter City's Barry invites Eric Morecombe to "get out of that!" The City players getting in on the joke are Cambell Crawford, Steve Stacey, Barry Rowan, Graham Parker, Bob Wilson, Mike Balson, John Wingate, Jimmy Giles, Fred Binney and Jimmy Blain.

the evening they all attended the Max Bygraves show. This included a visit behind stage where they enjoyed a chat-along-a-Max with the star of the show.

COMMERCIAL MATTERS

Thirty year old John Hillier was appointed as Exeter City's first ever Commercial Manager in October 1970. His target for the initial year was to raise £15,000. Mr Hillier stayed with Exeter until taking a similar appointment with his home town club, Colchester United. From there he joined Highland League side Keith, revitalising the Scottish non-league club's finances over several years, before returning south of the border again as Commercial Manager for Bristol City Football Club.

Mr Hillier worked out of offices situated in Blackboy Road. The club had bought the property shortly after his appointment as Commercial Manager, and converted it into a souvenir shop and offices. The official opening took place on 19th December 1970 with television sports presenter Gary Newbon cutting the ribbon.

During the early 1970s several Scottish clubs began selling Exeter City's weekly Golden Bonanza tickets. These included Scottish Leaguers Hibernian and Brechin City, and Lothian based side, Uphall Saints.

In February 1971 it was decided by the Exeter City Board of Directors to sever their connections with the Red and White Club, which had raised a substantial sum of money over the years for the parent club. The Red and White Club had been formed in 1962 by Les Kerslake, who was later to become chairman of Exeter City. It was a weekly competition which offered cash prizes to holders of lucky numbers. It was really an early scheme of the lottery which was to become such big business for Football Clubs in the 1980s. The break was made so that all fund raising schemes could be administered by City's Commercial Manager John Hillier. Exeter City director Wally Rice revealed that the Red and White Club had contributed £86,000 to Exeter City during the nineteen years of its existence. That figure was always disputed, for two years earlier, in March 1969, it had been reported in the local Press that the Red and White Club had contributed nearer £200,000.

Income from commercial activities was estimated by Exeter City director Wally Rice to have reached £17,000 a year by the end of 1971. He fully expected this to rise to £20,000 within the following twelve months. The large increase in fund raising activities had been attributed to the appointment of a Commercial Manager. Among items which had shown a marked increase in commercial income was perimeter ground advertising at St James's Park which then totalled over £600.

In October 1977 Exeter City launched their first ever monthly lottery. Tickets cost 20 pence, and at the end of each month, numbers were drawn for the prizes of £1,000, £500, £250, plus ten prizes of £50, and twenty prizes of £5. Three months after the launch of the lottery, such was its success, that a fortnightly draw was introduced.

The Vice President's Lounge was built in 1977 underneath the Grandstand, with boxer Alan Minter (later to become an Exeter City director), performing the official opening. The old boardroom and tea room was made into one large Vice Presidents' Lounge, with the annual fee for joining being £50. The V.P. Club has developed greatly since then, raising much needed finance and providing practical support on numerous occasions. The lounge area was re-built in 1990, and extended to provide catering facilities, with pre-match and after match meals being available.

CORNER KICKS

The rule allowing goals to be scored direct from corners was not introduced until 1924. However five years earlier in September 1919, the Gillingham versus Exeter City game saw three such efforts sail directly into the net only to be correctly disallowed! Connor of Gillingham twice achieved the feat of 'scoring' direct, and not to be outdone Exeter City's Charlie Lincoln also had a similar effort ruled out. Ironically the game ended goalless!

CROWD DEMONSTRATIONS

There have been a few crowd demonstrations at Exeter City over the years, notably more in recent times. The Exeter supporters are however perhaps a little more tolerant than many of their counterparts.

In the 1990/91 season following the FA sentence of banning club chairman Mr Ivor Doble from football for twelve months after alleged financial mismanagement, demonstrations at subsequent matches took place in support of Mr Doble and against the club president and a former member of the Board.

Another show of support for manager Frank Broome and club chairman Albert Line took place in October 1959. Mr Broome had offered to resign after a dispute among members of the Board. Supporters cheered wildly when a spectator paraded around the ground during the half-time interval against Crewe Alexandra carrying a placard that read, 'We Want Frank Broome.' A crowd of around 200 supporters gathered outside the Grandstand after the game to wait for another director who they thought was responsible for the unrest in the club. They were eventually moved on by police officers.

In December 1984 an alarming slump in the playing fortunes of the City, coupled with a takeover bid for the club by businessman Dan McCauley, prompted a supporters demonstration at the home match with Peterborough United. Supporters chanted for the removal of the Exeter chairman, Clifford Hill, from the Board of Directors to be replaced by Mr McCauley.

Four months later, with a new chairman, Byron Snell, in place, the City supporters again let their feelings be known towards him and the Board after the sacking of team manager Jim Iley. Around 200 supporters chanted in favour of Iley and against the Board. A petition protesting about the manager's sacking was handed to Mr Snell.

A group of Exeter City supporters demonstrated against the club's Board of Directors following the resignation of popular manager Terry Cooper. They marched across the St James's Park pitch during the half time interval at the pre-season friendly fixture with Millwall in August 1991, and took over the directors' box where they staged a noisy 'sit-in' for the rest of the game.

CROWD DISTURBANCES

The Crystal Palace team were pelted with mud as they left St James's Park to make their way to St David's Station after their match with Exeter City in September 1910. A group described as "rowdy youths" was involved in the incident. As a result the Football League ordered City to post notices around the ground warning followers of the club against any future disorder in and outside St James's Park.

The local Constabulary had to intervene at the Exeter City versus Aston Villa FA Cup tie in January 1914. An hour before the kick-off a fight was spotted between two spectators on the 'shilling bank'. The two persons involved were described as having 'a lively two rounds before the police got to them'! It is interesting to note that for this game which attracted an attendance of 11,000, there were fifty police officers on duty and two mounted constables were stationed outside the ground.

A spectator had to be restrained by several policemen and the two trainers as he invaded the pitch, and made an attempt to reach an Exeter City defender, during their FA Cup tie at Bournemouth in November 1946.

During Exeter City Reserves' 8-1 win over rivals Plymouth Argyle in a friendly match at St James's Park to raise funds for the Football League Jubilee Benevolent Fund, a spectator jumped over the railings onto the pitch. He was incensed by a series of heavy tackles on the City players. The spectator was quickly removed by a persuasive policeman.

A serious fracas took place in front of the Grandstand at the East Devon Divisional Cup Final played at St James's Park between The Loyals and The Royal Naval Transport Depot on 21st April 1945. After the final whistle, players indulged in a free for all. Spectators became involved and the referee was pushed to the ground. Several persons sustained injuries before order was eventually restored.

The Football Association ordered Exeter City to post notices around the ground and to be inserted in the match programme following incidents in the City versus Watford game on 6th November 1948 when missiles were thrown at referee Mr Wakley. Exeter forward Ron Johnston was ordered off in the same game for attempting to strike an opponent.

Warning notices had to again be posted in December 1955. This followed the home game with Aldershot when the visiting centre-half Charlie Billington was struck by a spectator as he entered the players' tunnel at the end of the match. Several other spectators had to be restrained during the unsavoury incident.

A section of the Exeter City crowd were far from happy with some of the challenges made by Bedford Town left back Adams in the match at St James's Park against the City Reserves in November 1954. At the end of the game, which Exeter won 1-0, a spectator had a tussle with the Bedford trainer who then signalled for a policeman to come to his aid. Adams also had to be escorted from the field to escape the wrath of the home supporters.

The following warning written by Exeter City secretary Dick Miller appeared in the match programme for the game against Swindon Town in October 1965: "At St James's Park we have always been proud of the conduct of our supporters, but more recently I have been concerned about some of the behaviour here. Such as the throwing of toilet rolls, slow hand clapping etc.

Let me give fair warning to those people inclined towards such action, that the police have strict instructions to remove from the ground anyone who is seen to throw toilet rolls onto the pitch."

During the first half of Exeter City's match at Newport County in February 1969 fifteen City supporters were ejected from the Somerton Park ground. A series of incidents took place including the throwing and smashing of a folding chair onto the surrounding cinder track. The following week the Exeter City Supporters Club sent a letter of apology to the Newport club expressing their disgust at the minority who had caused the trouble. After receiving a reply from Newport, the Supporters Club took the drastic step of stopping all coaches organised by themselves to future away fixtures.

Further incidents occurred on Exeter's visit to Newport the following season in August 1969. It was alleged by Newport County that Exeter fans had daubed slogans with red paint on gates, fences around the ground, and on two parked cars.

Wolverhampton Wanderers supporters disgraced themselves with scenes of wanton destruction before and after an FA Cup-tie at St James's Park in January 1978. A goal in the last three minutes had saved the First Division side from an humiliating defeat against Exeter City, the final result being 2-2.

Trouble began before the kick-off when the Wolves fans surged forward at the St James's Road end and smashed down the fencing and advertising boards, spilling onto the pitch. Twice more during the game they invaded the pitch, despite the blue line of police officers, who were simply overwhelmed by the sheer numbers.

Worse was to follow at the final whistle, when some of the Wolverhampton contingent raced the full length of the pitch to the Big Bank goal. They swung on the crossbar, snapping it in half, and then tried to wreck the goalposts. On leaving the ground the Wolves hooligans smashed windows of houses in Well Street and Victoria Street.

Sixty police officers were drafted in to deal with trouble before, during, and after the match between Exeter City and Bristol Rovers in January 1984. Twenty four fans were arrested, and six police constables were injured in various incidents, the worst of which occurred immediately after the final whistle, when the Rovers supporters charged across the pitch towards the Exeter City fans in the Cowshed.

A series of ugly incidents took place after Exeter City's home match with Cardiff City in November 1985. Visiting fans damaged Grandstand seats, invaded the pitch, broke a goal stanchion, and then tried to to get at their own team manager Alan Durban. He, along with his team, had to be escorted to the safety of the dressing rooms by the police. The fans then rampaged through

Sidwell Street and the High Street, scattering shoppers in their wake, breaking windows, and fighting with Exeter City supporters.

The following season, in September 1986, Cardiff supporters again caused havoc. Exeter City supporters were also blamed by the police for the violence which occurred before, during and after the game. Twenty one arrests were made as sporadic fighting broke out in the city centre and continued in the ground. Following this latest incident the Exeter Board of Directors immediately slapped a ban on all Cardiff City fans from the ground for future matches and stated that any Exeter supporters involved and caught by the police would also be banned from St James's Park.

The number of arrests made by the Exeter police at St James's Park during the 1987/88 season was twenty four, from a total attendance figure of 56,264. There were eighteen Exeter City supporters arrested at St James's Park, and six away supporters. A further forty seven arrests were made outside the ground for football related offences. No fewer than forty of those forty seven were made in the city centre before the Exeter City versus Cardiff City fixture. The local police were full of praise for the measures that had been introduced by Exeter City Football Club, such as the closed circuit television cameras, and the Cowshed membership scheme, which had greatly helped them reduce cases of football hooliganism.

CUSHIONS

A note regarding the hire of cushions appeared in the Exeter City versus Leicester City FA Cup tie programme in January 1937. It read: "Cushions may be hired at the cost of 2d. It is hoped that everyone will assist by treating the cushions with care. It will be of great assistance to the Committee for everyone to hand their cushions back to the stewards at the end of the match. These cushions should never be thrown at the referee or linesmen during the game as they have no time to use them, and the thrower may get a boomerang. The cushions will be kept in a good dry condition and will be handed out at the entrances to the Grandstand as you enter."

In September 1969 the referee stopped the match at St James's Park between Exeter City and Port Vale whilst he ordered an announcement to be made over the public address system. This warned spectators that action would be taken if any further incidents occurred. An Exeter supporter in the Grandstand had thrown a cushion onto the pitch, showing his disgust at the referee's offside decision against a City player!

DEAD OR ALIVE

Frank Broome, the Exeter City manager, had a nasty shock in December 1968. The Australian newspaper, *The Sydney Sun*, reported that Frank had been killed in a Motorway accident. There was even a one minute silence held

Frank Broome returned to take over as manager of Exeter City for a second spell in 1967. He is seen pictured with the team of 1968/69. Back row (L to R) Alan Pinkney, Campbell Crawford, Cecil Smyth, Jimmy Blain. Middle Row (L to R) John Corr, Dermot Curtis, Mike Balson, Peter Shearing, Brian Sharples, John Kirkham, Keith Harvey, Bert Edwards (trainer). Front row (L to R) Keith Whatling, John Mitten, Frank Broome, John Newman, David Pleat (completing a trio of football league managers).

in his memory at the New South Wales Federation Annual General Meeting, for Frank had been the coach at a Sydney based club until returning to Exeter City.

The newspaper however had to admit its mistake when a letter was sent to them by friends of Mr Broome pointing out that he was indeed alive and well. And Frank Broome's reaction to this? "I am in a position to deny the story," he said!

DEVON LEAGUE

Exeter City were among the clubs who attended a meeting at Plymouth in November 1983 to discuss the possible formation of a Devon County League to commence in the 1984/85 season. They gave a firm commitment along with five other clubs to join the proposed league if it was formed. Other clubs represented at the meeting were, Alphington, Crediton United, Cullompton Rangers, Ilfracombe Town, Ivybridge, Plymstock, Topsham Town, Torquay United, and Weston Mill Oak Villa.

DEVON PROFESSIONAL BOWL

After several years lapse the Devon Professional Bowl was played for again in 1984. As Exeter City had last won the trophy in 1974, they were assumed by the Devon County Football Association to have the trophy in safe keeping. Panic stricken City officials could not recall where the said trophy was however! The County FA secretary remarked that a professional club like Exeter City should surely be proudly displaying the trophy in a cabinet at the ground. They were not amused at the thought of the possible loss of the trophy.

A thorough search of St James's Park was instigated. The mystery of the missing Devon Professional Bowl was solved! City groundsman Sonny Clarke put everybody's minds at rest when he produced the trophy which had been stored in his shed! It had been put there by Sonny for safe keeping when work was being carried out on moving the commercial offices to the ground.

This was not the only item to be found in Sonny's shed! For several old framed photographs were later discovered lying there including prewar team photographs. Exeter City Football Club photograph collector, Dave Fisher of Exmouth, quickly 'rescued' these precious historical records, and cleaned the frames, some of which were in a filthy condition. The photographs were then handed back to the club. They were last heard of – resting back in the groundsman's shed! They can't be still there – can they?

DIDO THE SEAGULL

The legend of 'Dido the Seagull' is synonymous with the history of Exeter City Football Club. The bird first appeared swooping low over St James's Park, and perched on the crossbar during the Club's famous run to the FA Cup quarter final in 1930/31. It was quickly adopted by the City supporters as being a lucky omen or mascot. If 'Dido' appeared, then City were supposedly certain of a victory. Further seagulls, all of course called 'Dido', have appeared since!

'Dido Mania' occurred when the City were drawn at home to Leeds United in the fifth round of the FA Cup in February 1931. Story has it that a supporter who was jostled whilst waiting patiently in a queue to get into St James's Park said, "Careful mate! I don't want my pocket squashed." Putting his hand into his pocket he produced a large tasty mackerel, which he intended throwing to 'Dido' when he appeared!

After Exeter City's run in the 1930/31 FA Cup competition was ended by Sunderland in the quarter-final, it was reported in the local Press in May 1931 that 'Dido' had not been seen for some weeks over St James's Park, but three seagulls were seen to fly over Wembley Stadium on Cup Final afternoon. It couldn't be – could it?

In January 1937 before a home fourth round FA Cup tie with Leicester City, a seagull encircled St James's Park, and was described as being as a 'Descendant of Dido'. City went on to win the game 3-1. In the very next round at First Division Preston North End, City supporters paraded a stuffed 'Dido' on a pole through the streets of the Lancashire town much to the amusement of the locals. Unfortunately, the City team were 'stuffed' as well, as they lost 5-3!

'Dido Junior' was caught by three Exeter City supporters living in Drewsteignton in November 1946. It was tamed, and put through a course of special training in the hope that the bird would bring City luck in their FA Cup tie at Bournemouth. It was taken to the game by road and presented to City captain Harry Hanford just before the kick-off. Exeter lost 4-2, Hanford gave away a penalty, and 'Dido Junior' was described as going into permanent and honourable retirement! But did it?

Another stuffed 'Dido' (could it be the same one as in 1937?), this time displayed in a glass case, was offered to Exeter City in September 1961 by Miss E.P. Hill-Willis of Heavitree Road, Exeter. She thought that the bird, if resident at St James's Park, bearing in mind its illustrious past, may have brought the club luck. It is not known however if the City did find a home for the bird. The chances are they didn't for Exeter finished eighteenth in Division Four and were knocked out of the FA Cup by non-league Dartford.

DIRECTORS

Exmouth resident, Mrs Jenne, a daughter of former Exeter City director Mr F. Nicholls, fondly recalls that the directors' wives in the 1920s and 1930s retired on cold days to a house overlooking the ground in St James's Road so that they could watch the game in warm surroundings. The house was owned by an Exeter City director.

She adds that Mr Nicholls was a non-smoker, and also teetotal. Whilst the rest of the directors partook of half-time and full-time alcoholic refreshments, he would join the players in the City dressing room! He was at the time probably more involved with the players than any of the other directors were.

The unusual step of advertising for directors to join the Exeter City Board was taken in October 1966. The club placed the following advertisement in the *Express and Echo* newspaper: 'A vacancy occurs for a director to join the Board of Exeter City Football Club. Qualifications include investment in the club and a desire to play an integral part in its life.'

Mike Holladay became Exeter City's first paid Commercial Director in 1990. His brief was to promote the commercial activities of the club, as well as continuing his involvement with the day to day running of Exeter City. He originally joined the Exeter City Board of Directors after selling his family business, and became increasingly involved at the City on a daily basis. Holladay was later to become club secretary.

DISCIPLINARY MATTERS

Exeter City were ordered to appear before a Football Association Disciplinary Committee in August 1983, after being named as one of nine clubs with an unsatisfactory disciplinary record on the field during the previous season. The club were fined £250.

DRUM AND MONKEY

The Drum and Monkey public house played a major part in the formation of Exeter City Football Club. The pub stood in Sidwell Street roughly on the site of the present Odeon Cinema, and it was there that a team was formed by local lads called St Sidwell's United. The Drum and Monkey was actually called the Foresters Arms, but was always referred to by the former name by the regulars who frequented the hostelry. St Sidwell's United played their matches at the Horse Show Field in Mount Pleasant. No teams of comparable age could match them and they then decided to challenge local rivals Exeter United who were playing at St James's Field. St Sidwell's won 3-1, and Exeter United later faded into obscurity. St Sidwell's then took over at the St James's ground, and changed their name to Exeter City in 1904.

EVERTON

Exeter City have never met Everton in a Football League match, but have, however, played them three times, twice in friendly fixtures at St James's Park and more recently in an FA Cup tie at Goodison Park. The first game took place in 1954, shortly after floodlights had first been installed at St James's Park, with the visitors winning 4-0. Everton again visited Exeter for a pre-season friendly in the early 1980s.

Exeter made their one and only appearance at Everton's Goodison Park ground in a third round FA Cup-tie in January 1986 when they narrowly lost 1-0 in front of a crowd of 22,726.

FA CUP

The first venture into the FA Cup competition by Exeter City in October 1908 was described as being: "farcical in the extreme". Their opponents at St James's Park were Weymouth, who trailed by 10-0 at the interval. They conceded four further goals in the second half, such was the supremacy held by Exeter. James 'Daisy' Bell scored six of the goals, while Andy McGuigan netted another four. Levi Copestake scored two more, Bob Watson and Fred Parnell helped themselves to a goal each.

In the following round Exeter were drawn away to Kingswood Rovers, who played at the Chequers ground, Warmley, Bristol. Kingswood offered to switch the match to St James's Park, but the City directors declined saying that the reserve match against Looe in the Plymouth and District League, scheduled to be played that afternoon, was likely to prove just as much an attraction for their supporters as Kingswood! The tie went ahead at Kingswood, with City winning 2-0.

Nelson Football Club objected to the Football Association regarding their FA Cup tie against Exeter City in December 1910. Because the St James's Park pitch was too small, and not being of sufficient length to stage cup ties, City having been drawn at home offered to play the game at the County Ground in St Thomas. Nelson, however, objected saying that they were not bound by the rules to play on any alternative venue and that Exeter City should therefore concede ground advantage. The Football Association agreed and the tie went ahead at Nelson, but the story had a happy ending for Exeter as they won 4-3, scoring three goals in a five minute spell.

Exeter City made a wasted trip to non-league Barnet for a first round tie on Saturday 27th November 1948. A crowd of around 2,000 were in the sloping Underhill ground when the match was called off just fifteen minutes before kick-off because of fog. It was of particular disappointment to the two coach loads of City supporters who had travelled overnight to attend the game, and around 300 Exeter fans who had similarly made the journey from the West Country by a special rail excursion. The match eventually took place a week later, with Exeter City winning 6-2, the first City goal being scored after just ten seconds through Archie Smith.

The Nuneaton Borough party of officials and players stayed at the Cranford Hotel in Exmouth prior to their third round FA Cup tie at Exeter City in January 1950. The licensee of the Cranford Hotel was Wing Commander J. Edwards who was also the president of the Exmouth branch of the Grecians Association. The team arrived in Exmouth on the Thursday, and trained on the Exmouth Town pitch at the Maer Cricket field. They then attended a pantomime in the Church Hall at Exmouth the following evening. An official welcome was given to the Nuneaton party by the Chairman of the Exmouth Urban District Council. One of their supporters cycled to St James's Park all the way from Nuneaton, leaving his home at 3.30 p.m. on the Friday afternoon. For the record, Nuneaton lost the game against the City 3-0.

Video cameras are now taken for granted, but for City's third round cup tie against Stoke City a cine camera was used for the first time to record events. The camera, along with a projector, had been given to the club by Exeter City director Albert Line with the idea that matches could be filmed and then played back to show up tactical errors. Local photographic expert Eric Keen was given the task of filming and editing the game.

After Exeter City had been dumped out of the FA Cup at the first round stage in 1984 by non-league Enfield, losing 3-0 in the replay on the London club's ground, chairman Clifford Hill blasted: "In fifteen years at the club I have never publicly criticised an Exeter City team performance, but this evening our players humiliated themselves, this club, and the city of Exeter."

Exeter had, three days earlier, drawn 2-2 with Enfield in the first meeting between the two sides at St James's Park. Manager Jim Iley added: "This result just goes to show how bad a team we are."

FA ENQUIRY

The Football Association conducted an enquiry into the affairs of Exeter City Football Club in 1912 following certain complaints made to them by three of the directors. The enquiry took place at the Great Western Hotel, St David's, Exeter on 1st June 1912. The City club had to furnish their account books to the FA for the enquiry to be prepared. It had been no secret for some time that there was a split among the Board of Directors at St James's Park and it was because of this that matters were reported to the FA.

The charges laid against certain directors and Exeter City concerned illegal bonuses paid to players for winning matches. It was understood that details of this happening were reported to the FA by City director, Mr T. Oliver, with statements being signed by fellow directors, Mr W.H. Cook, and Mr W. Fenwick. The bonuses were alleged to have been paid during the 1908/09, 1910/11 and 1911/12 seasons.

The result of the FA Commission of enquiry was that the cash book kept by Exeter City Football Club was found to be incomplete, and generally the books were not being kept in a satisfactory condition.

Former Exeter City chairman, Captain Harvey, had admitted to the enquiry

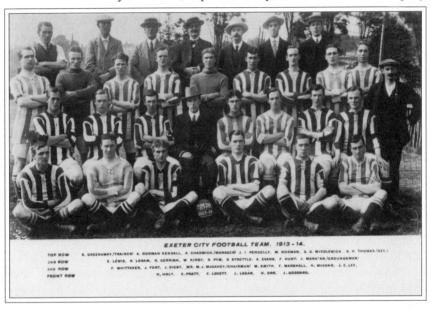

EXETER CITY FOOTBALL TEAM. 1913 – 14.

TOP ROW   S. GREENAWAY, (TRAINER) A. NORMAN KENDALL, A. CHADWICK, (MANAGER) J. I. PENGELLY, W. NORMAN, G. A. MIDDLEWICK, S. H. THOMAS (SEC.)
2ND ROW   E. LEWIS, R. LORAM, R. GERRISH, W. KIRBY, R. PYM, S. STRETTLE, A. EVANS, F. HUNT, J. MANA'AN, (GROUNDSMAN)
3RD ROW   F. WHITTAKER, J. FORT, J. RIGBY, MR. M. J. McGAHEY, (CHAIRMAN) W. SMITH, F. MARSHALL, H. McCANN, J. C. LEE,
FRONT ROW   H. HOLT, C. PRATT, F. LOVETT, J. LAGAN, H. ORR, J. GODDARD.

that bonuses had indeed been paid. It was further admitted by the club that bonuses had been paid to players for the FA Cup ties with Reading in the 1910/11 season. A portion of the gate receipts from the Exeter City versus New Brompton Southern League match played on 9th September 1911 had been put aside as a reserve fund, and was not shown in the accounts. The enquiry found that Exeter City directors, Messrs Cook, Fenwick, Parkhouse, Oliver and Thomas were well aware of this happening, without the knowledge of the remaining directors. The charge made by Mr Oliver was that this was done to pay bonuses. As soon as this came to the knowledge of the then chairman, Mr McGahey, he brought it before the directors' meeting and the practice was discontinued, the money being placed in club funds. No bonuses were paid, and no illegitimate use of the money was made thereafter.

The FA Commission approved of the action taken by Mr McGahey and the other directors and censured Messrs. Cook, Fenwick, Parkhouse, Oliver, and Thomas for their improper and irregular action. The commission were satisfied that the books were not entered up to date, nor kept in accordance with FA regulations. They therefore ordered Exeter City Football Club to immediately complete the books in a satisfactory manner and levied a fine of £20 upon the club.

In the course of the enquiry the Commission found that Mr T. Oliver, who did not report the irregularities until eight months after the date, though himself aware at the time, had been the primary cause of dissension among the Exeter City Board of Directors. In the interests of the club the Commission ordered Mr Oliver to be suspended from acting as a director of Exeter City, or be connected with the club in any other official capacity.

It was regarded by many that the whole affair was possibly unique in so much that the director who drew the Football Association's attention to the alleged irregularities in the first place, be the only person who was suspended.

Another FA enquiry into the club's affairs took place in 1990, when allegations of financial mismanagement were made. It was reported that former chairman Byron Snell had spoken to the Football Association expressing his concern at the alleged occurrence. This was with regards to a grant obtained from the Football Grounds Improvement Trust in connection with essential safety works being carried out at St James's Park. The then club chairman Ivor Doble admitted that there had been an overpayment in the grant received of around £27,000, but he had repaid this to the Trust.

The whole incident brought a very bad press for Exeter City, but to the credit of the manager, Terry Cooper and his players, they battled on gamely, when it was obvious they had to be affected by the adverse publicity and uncertainty surrounding the club. Amazingly City won promotion by ending the season as Fourth Division Champions. The uncertainty was heightened when the FA ordered an enquiry into the club's affairs. In the meantime, Byron Snell, along with two other directors, Geno Vece (who actually resigned from the Board), and Archie Gooch were removed as directors at a special meeting of shareholders.

It was revealed at the same meeting that the contractors who had carried out safety work at St James's Park made a refund on the original estimate for the job as a form of sponsorship. This totalled around 25 per cent of the total cost of the work. The club were obviously delighted with this gesture, but on talking to their accountants it was pointed out that as City had in fact claimed a grant towards the work, the refund may have contravened this. Mr Doble then contacted the Football Grounds Improvement Trust and repaid them a sum of money at a meeting held with the trusts chairman in Glasgow.

After a lengthy investigation the FA brought charges in December 1990 against Exeter City Football Club, the chairman, Ivor Doble, finance director

Murray Couch, commercial director Mike Holladay, and former Board member Archie Gooch. A fine of £9,500 including costs was levied against the club. Mr Couch was suspended as a director for six months, and fined a total of £5,000. Mr Gooch was suspended for three months, and fined a total of £4,000. Mr Holladay was fined a total of £3,000. The chairman, Mr Doble, was suspended for twelve months and fined a total of £7,000. He appealed against the decision three months later, but the brief fifteen minute hearing upheld their original verdict.

FATHER AND SON

Charlie Miller made 274 Football league appearances for Exeter City between 1926 and 1936. A full back who has been described as one of the club's finest, he later became assistant trainer at St James's Park in 1947. His son, Dick, was appointed secretary of Exeter City in 1965. Dick tragically lost his life in a car accident three years later.

Barry Redwood made his debut for Exeter City in a Football League Cup tie in 1963, and his son Toby played his first match for the club twenty seven years later. Barry, a forward, made his debut in Exeter's 1-0 defeat in a second round tie at Hull City in September 1963. Toby, a defender, played his first game in the 1-0 Third Division home win over local rivals Torquay United in September 1991.

Another father and son combination to represent Exeter City were the Harrowers. Bill Harrower made eighty five League appearances for the City between 1948 and 1952, whilst his son, Steve, signed for Exeter in 1983 from Dawlish Town. Steve remained at St James's Park for seven years before moving to Yeovil Town.

Terry Cooper was appointed manager of Exeter City in May 1988. He signed his son Mark, a midfielder from Bristol City, in September 1989. Terry resigned as manager of Exeter at the start of the 1991/92 season, and moved to Birmingham City as their manager. Within a month Terry had returned to St James's Park in September 1991 to re-sign his son Mark for his new club.

FINANCE

Money was the root of most problems even as early as 1911. Collections were taken for a Summer Wage Fund to meet the Exeter City players' wages during the close season break. At one stage it was suggested to manager Arthur Chadwick that no players were to be re-engaged until August so that the club would not have to find any money to pay their wages. Chadwick quickly dismissed this idea, for it would have been impossible at such a late stage to sign new players, the best having already been fixed up with other clubs by then. The collection raised over £200, half of the total coming at a public meeting called to discuss the situation.

The situation was no different the following year. To help offset the cost of the players' summer wages in 1912, a friendly fixture was played against Plymouth Argyle in March of that year at St James's Park with all the receipts going into the wages fund.

In 1920 the accounts presented at the club's AGM showed a working profit of just over £1,084 on the year. Total gross receipts came to £10,509. Wages accounted for £3,361, while travelling expenses totalled £1,205.

Percy Varco, one of the heroes of Exeter City's FA Cup run to the quarter-final of 1930/31, recalled how the club's directors told them afterwards that all the players would have to take a pay cut! Varco, a goalscoring forward, who died at the age of 78 in February 1982, said that the players were summoned to a meeting with the directors. They were told that a pay cut of £1 per week was to be implemented due to the recession of the early 1930s. Varco was then earning the princely sum of £7 per week at Exeter having been signed from Norwich City. Varco felt that it was almost as if the directors were punishing the players for losing to Sunderland in the quarter-final. In his opinion the directors ruined the side, which resulted in many of the players moving on to other clubs.

Varco was transferred to Brighton and Hove Albion, and later played for Queen's Park Rangers. An injury ended his playing career, and Varco retired to Fowey in his native Cornwall where he spent thirty years as a Fowey town councillor, twice becoming the town mayor.

It was reported at the 1949 annual meeting of the shareholders of Exeter City Football Club that receipts for the year had totalled a record £30,321. The cost of running the club was quoted as f530 per week all the year round. Twelve months later City director Les Seward said that the club needed regular home attendances of 12–14,000 to enable Exeter City to be run on an economic basis.

It was announced at the commencement of the 1960/61 season that players who made the Exeter City first team would earn £18 per week, with an additional £2 paid as an incentive if the side were in the top four of the Fourth Division.

The 1960/61 season, however, saw Exeter City slip into deep financial trouble which threatened the very existence of the club. Chairman George Gillin said in January 1961 that it was difficult to say where the wages were coming from on a week to week basis, and that the City had acute financial problems. By December 1961 the financial position of the club had obviously not improved, for it was expressed by the Board of Directors at the Annual General Meeting that the backlog of debts was causing very real concern.

Brighton and Hove Albion reported Exeter City to the Football League in October 1962 for non-payment of a final transfer fee instalment of £1,400.

This was in respect of player-manager Glen Wilson's move from Brighton to Exeter in June 1960.

A new incentive was introduced by Exeter City for players prior to the commencement of the 1963/64 season. For every 1,000 spectators through the St James's Park turnstiles over and above 5,000, the players received an extra £1 per thousand. City winger Graham Rees spoke on behalf of the players saying that they had suggested the scheme to the directors who were quite happy to agree to it.

The Exeter City squad that won promotion for the first time in the club's history, in 1963/64. Standing (L to R) Jack Edwards (manager), Keith Harvey, Cecil Smyth, Alan Barnett, Dave Hancock, Les MacDonald, Des Anderson. Seated (L to R) Dermot Curtis, Arnold Mitchell, Adrian Thorne, Graham Rees, Derek Grace, Alan Banks.

At the shareholders meeting in August 1963, Exeter City chairman Reg Rose told them: "I have never seen or heard of any business in a worse mess than when I took over at St James's Park. The club was at rock bottom and it was touch and go whether we would be able to carry on."

The cost of promotion for the first time in the club's history in 1963/64 was £11,000. This was the loss incurred by Exeter during the season as revealed in the club's accounts. Whilst gate receipts increased from £12,114 in the 1962/63 season to £22,704, on the debit side, transfer fees and players removal expenses had accounted for over £13,000. Wages and salaries increased to £30,972. The club's total deficiency stood at £45,052.

Club chairman Gerald Vallance expressed a far from optimistic note about the future of Exeter City in November 1974. He revealed that the club were losing £300 per week, and whilst he was confident that they would see the 1974/75 season out, the following twelve months was a different matter. Exeter needed attendances at the Park of a minimum of 4,000 to enable the club to break even, but the average home gate was in fact only 3,209 at that particular time.

The club's average wage bill was £450 per week, and this together with other outgoings brought the weekly expenditure to around £1,300 a week. In return the average gate receipts totalled around £1,000 gross.

The actual loss for the 1974/75 season was £30,909, prompting Mr Vallance to say: "It is certain that the next six months are going to be extremely difficult financially, but if we can see our way through this period, then I believe the future could be much brighter."

Alan Beer

The club's financial director, Ian Webb, revealed, in February 1982, that the cost of running Exeter City was £20,000 a month. He added that with the average Third Division player earning £10,000 per year, even the then small playing staff at Exeter was really more than could be afforded.

Exeter City were in a deep financial crisis by September 1982. In a drastic attempt to save money, four members of the backroom staff were told that their services were being dispensed with. They were coach and former player Alan Beer, Youth Development Officer Chris Davey, chief youth scout Roger Quintin, and long serving secretary Pat Wakeham who had been at the club for ten years. At the same time financial director Ian Webb also resigned from the Board. It was believed that these measures had to be taken after the club's bankers met with the club. The scrapping of the successful Youth Policy was another possibility to save cash.

The local Press described Exeter City Football Club as 'tottering on the brink of bankruptcy'. Vice-Chairman Clifford Hill who admitted that the club had been in daily contact with their bankers said: "We have no panic. Just realisation of facts. We have had a crisis which we think we have averted by prompt action. We can see a glimmer of light at the end of the tunnel."

It was reported in December 1983 that Exeter City had lost £92,923 in the previous financial year. The club's overall deficit stood at £239,219. Wages and signing on fees had accounted for £287,815, transfer fees £12,000, and travelling and hotel expenses £26,235. On the plus side the commercial department had raised a total of £93,250 during the year. By March 1985 however, the club's financial position had worsened considerably. Exeter City announced that they were £304,283 in the red at the year ending 31st May 1984.

Accounts released for the 1987/88 season showed that Exeter City's overall deficit stood at £509,734. The club did however report a profit on the season of just over £12,000. Expenditure for the season rose to £505,446, whilst income totalled £517,642.

FIRE

A disaster which could have been comparable to the fire that destroyed the Grandstand at St James's Park in November 1925 was narrowly averted thanks to prompt actions of director Billy Crawshaw and Grecians official Les Kerslake. A Board meeting had taken place at the ground on Thursday 8th December 1960, when the two gentlemen, leaving after everyone else, noticed smoke coming from under a locked door. Mr Crawshaw smashed a wooden panel to break into the boardroom, where he and Mr Kerslake discovered that the wall panelling was alight. Between them they managed to put out the fire, without too much damage being caused. It was believed that the fire was caused by a smouldering cigarette end in a waste paper basket.

A small fire broke out in the main Grandstand during the first half of Darlington's match with Exeter City in September 1972. It was quickly extinguished with buckets of water. The fire was described as being the only thing of any note in an otherwise boring first forty five minutes of football!

Damage estimated to be in the region of £10,000 was caused by a fire at the Centre Spot Social Club in June 1989. The fire started amongst chairs and tables that had been stacked outside the building, but it quickly spread inside the club and along the roof.

FIRSTS

The first ever match played by Exeter City took place on Saturday 10th September 1904, an East Devon League fixture played at St James's Field against the 110th Battery. City won 2-1 watched by a crowd of 600, with the first ever goal being scored by Eveleigh. The other goal came from, appropriately Sidney Thomas, who had been one of the 'leading lights' behind the formation of the club.

Exeter City's first ever professional was Jack Banks, who was signed from Plymouth Argyle in 1907. He had appeared in the FA Cup Final for West

Bromwich Albion in 1895. He died at his Barrow home in January 1947.

The first ever FA representative match to be staged at St James's Park was between an FA Amateur XI and a Combined Universities XI, on Wednesday 24th February 1937, which the students won 4-1.

The numbering of players shirts was believed to have been first seen at Exeter on 19th August 1939 when the City played Plymouth Argyle in a friendly to raise funds for the Football League Jubilee Fund. New standard size Football League crossbars and goalposts were also used for the first time.

The first Board of Directors of Exeter City, following the resumption of football after the Second World War, was elected on 28th April 1945 as follows:
Mr S. Thomas (Chairman), Mr F. Cottey (Vice-Chairman), and Messrs. A.T. Ford, C.V.H. Hill, J. Lake, F.P. Nicholls, J.G.R. Orchard, J. Rigby, and J.G. Warne.

The first match to be played on a Good Friday at St James's Park was in March 1948. Bournemouth and Boscombe Athletic were the visitors, the result being 1-1, in a game watched by 15,833 spectators.

FISHING

Southend United were disappointed with the 4,000 attendance for their Third Division South match against Exeter City in October 1921.

Club officials explained that due to an important fishing competition held on the same day on Southend Pier the attendance was bound to suffer. It was estimated that no fewer than 1,500 anglers took part. Southend lost 1-0 to the City and the match report stated that the anglers on the pier were probably treated to more entertainment watching the crabs being caught than those who attended the game!

FLIGHTS

The Mayor of Exeter, Mr R.J. Rew, and several other city dignitaries, made the first ever civic flight from Exeter Airport on Saturday 27th August 1938. They flew to Exeter City's Third Division South fixture at Cardiff. They were joined by their counterparts, from the city of Cardiff, in the directors' box at Ninian Park for the game which ended in a 2-1 win for Exeter.

The civic party, which also included former Exeter City player, Billy Crawshaw, made the flight in a De Haviland Rapide aircraft which originally belonged to the Duke of Windsor. They left Exeter Airport at 11.15 a.m. arriving in Cardiff less than an hour later.

Perhaps the first ever group of supporters to charter an aircraft for a match at St James's Park were those of Nuneaton Borough. Around one hundred fans paid the return air fare of £9.10s so that they could attend their club's FA Cup replay at Exeter City in December 1967. The game ended in another draw

– 0-0, with a second replay taking place at Bristol City's Ashton Gate ground, which Exeter won 1-0.

A group of around one hundred Exeter City supporters flew aboard a chartered Boeing 737 airliner to the club's FA Cup replay at Norwich in January 1990. The cost was £130 per person, which included the flight, on board meal, and transfer to Norwich City's Carrow Road ground. The party left Exeter Airport at 4 p.m., arriving in Norwich an hour later. The return flight arrived back in Exeter at around midnight. A plane had also been chartered earlier in the season for City's Football League Cup tie at Sunderland.

FLOODLIGHTS

Arc Lights were used for training at St James's Park for the first time on Thursday 31st October 1946, when on a floodlit pitch City's part-time professionals and amateurs were able to go through their paces. This innovation was deemed to be a big success.

EXETER CITY FOOTBALL CLUB
Official Programme
PRICE 3ᵈ
Opening Floodlit Match
EXETER CITY
VERSUS
PLYMOUTH ARGYLE
TUESDAY, 3rd MARCH, 1953

A floodlit match was due to be played for the first time at St James's Park between Exeter City and Plymouth Argyle on Tuesday 3rd March 1951, but the game never started because forty five minutes before kick-off, the ground became shrouded in fog. Queues of supporters outside the ground were naturally disappointed at the news. However, a few walked the short distance to the Odeon Cinema in Sidwell Street to watch the Charlie Chaplin film, appropriately named, 'Limelight'.

Argyle's journey to Exeter was not entirely wasted for they were entertained by the City directors at a dinner held in the Queen's Hotel. Edgar Dobell, a Plymouth Argyle director, said that he thought floodlit football was here to stay and, whilst it was a novelty at that present time, it was like a beard – sure to grow.

The *Express and Echo* newspaper report of the official 'switch-on' of the St James's Park floodlights, which eventually took place against Plymouth Argyle on 9th March 1953, described the occasion: "The lights were brilliant,

Plymouth Argyle dazzled, Exeter City were eclipsed. No fault could be found with the floodlights. Play could be easily followed from all parts of the ground."

Before the match, which Argyle won 3-0, there was a short opening ceremony when the Exeter City Board of Directors thanked the Grecians Association for defraying the cost of the floodlights.

The Exeter City Colts team made history on Tuesday 8th December 1953, when they took part in the first ever Exeter and District League match to be played under floodlights. Their opponents at St James's Park were the Torquay side, Chelston, who obviously didn't shine as City won 5-1.

Floodlit football was still very much in its infancy even in March 1956. Commenting after his team had just lost 6-1 to Exeter City Reserves at St James's Park in a Southern League fixture, the Llanelli manager said that it had been the first time they had played under floodlights and the dazzle had affected his players.

The Exeter City versus Watford match on 10th November 1956 was the first Saturday afternoon game at St James's Park to be played partially under floodlights. Both clubs agreed that the lights would be turned on when ever necessary.

By 1963 the set of floodlights installed ten years earlier needed replacing. In December of that year, club chairman Reg Rose said: "There is no doubt that the floodlights must be the number one priority. We know it will be expensive to replace the lights – at least £8,000 and that is without the steelwork. The modern day four pylon corner system is probably not for

Exeter City in view of the present construction of the ground. It is more likely we will have to go for an extension of the present system with floodlights along the top of the Grandstand."

By October 1964, the floodlights which had by now deteriorated rapidly, were brought to the notice of the Football League by visiting clubs who had complained about them. There were great patches of darkness in each corner of the ground and strips of shadows across the centre. Indeed as early as 1959, City goalkeeper George Hunter had pointed out that when the opposition took a corner at night he had to guess the flight of the ball!

The outcome of other club's complaints was that Exeter City were ordered by the League not to use the lights until they were brought up to standard. Some new floodlighting equipment had in fact been delivered to St James's Park, but it was not expected that the new set would be operational for another two months.

Exeter immediately appealed to the Football League to be allowed to use the lights for two further midweek home fixtures, until the new set was in place. The League agreed to this, but instructed City to specially clean and overhaul the existing set for their next scheduled midweek match with Brentford. A report on the lights would be submitted to the League after the game by the referee.

Ironically, the floodlights suffered a power failure as Brentford ran out onto the pitch five minutes before the appointed 7.15 p.m. kick-off! A cable fault plunged half the ground in darkness. A frantic call was made to the South Western Electricity Board, who arrived at the ground, and had the lights working again by 7.40 p.m. Out came the players and the match officials – and then? – the lights went out again! The referee decided to wait until 8 p.m. If the floodlights were not working by then he would have no alternative but to call the game off.

Happily they did work again, and the match kicked off at 8 p.m. During the forty five minute delay most of the City supporters stood in darkness not knowing what was going on, for the loudspeaker system also failed. Someone in their wisdom did walk around the ground with a message chalked on a board, but of course it was so dark that no-one could read it!

The referee had obviously still not been impressed with the lights, however, for two days later the Football League once again contacted the City and placed a ban on the system until the new one was operational.

Exeter had made progress towards the new system being installed with two additional poles being placed at either end of the ground for floodlights in addition to the lights along the top of the Grandstand and the Cowshed. The ban, however, did mean that Saturday afternoon games would have to kick-off at the earlier time of 2.30 p.m.

The new floodlights were officially switched-on with a friendly fixture against the full Arsenal first team, including seven international players, on

Wednesday 2nd December 1964. An attendance of 11,507 saw the Gunners win 4-1, with Frank McClintock scoring a hat-trick. The lights were described as being brighter than those at Wembley Stadium! Guest of honour at the game was former Exeter City and Arsenal winger Cliff Bastin.

The floodlighting system was updated in 1979, and again during the 1991/92 season bringing the lights up to a Second Division standard. Several match officials had previously pointed out to Exeter that the floodlights were not really up to standard, and the club decided to renew the system, with the assistance of a Football Grounds Improvement Trust grant, before any official complaints were made to the Football League.

FOOD POISONING

Exeter City had a miserable start to the New Year in 1949. They lost 3-0 at Norwich City, but the scoreline does not tell the whole story, for Exeter only just managed to raise a team, and several who took to the field were far from fit. Their troubles began when right half and captain, Harry Bartholomew developed sciatica on the journey to East Anglia, and no fewer than eight other players were taken ill on the morning of the match with suspected food poisoning. Players were given medication in an attempt to get them through the game, but nevertheless it was still necessary to play 38-year-old trainer, Jimmy Gallagher, at centre-half. In the circumstances, City did well to restrict the final score to 3-0.

FOUND

A rather unusual item was found in the Grandstand following Exeter City's 1-1 draw with Southport in September 1963. A set of dentures! Four days later, the dentures still remained unclaimed.

An Exeter City supporter (and Exeter Sunday Football League player) lost his contact lens in the excitement of seeing Nicky Jennings scoring in a match during the 1974/75 season. Some supporters stayed behind after the final whistle to scour the terraces where the unfortunate fellow had stood. Then at 9.45 p.m., thirty minutes after the end of the game, the lens turned up. It was found in the corner of his eye!

FOURTH DIVISION

As one of the founder members of the Fourth Division in 1958, Exeter City soon began to realise that there would be a good deal of travelling and expense involved after years of Third Division South football. Even before the season had started City were none too pleased with the prospect of having to play at Darlington on the Saturday and at Barrow the following Monday night. Secretary George Gilbert arranged for the team to travel by train (no motorways then!), to both matches which involved the following schedule:

Friday 29th August: Depart Exeter 10.30 a.m. Arrive Darlington 8.23 p.m. Saturday 30th August: Darlington versus Exeter City. Sunday 31st August: Depart Darlington 2.35 p.m. Arrive Barrow 10.30 p.m. Monday 1st September: Barrow versus Exeter City. Tuesday 2nd September: Depart Barrow 9 a.m. Arrive Exeter 7.50 p.m.

So what of the costings for that Northern 'safari'? Exeter expected to receive £100 as their share of the gate receipts from the Darlington match, but only around £50 from the poorer supported Barrow. Rail fares for the City party consisting of one director, manager Frank Broome, trainer Eddie Nash and twelve players totalled £84, whilst the hotel bills for four nights stay came to at least £70. In addition there was the cost of meals for five days. Exeter therefore estimated that they would make a loss on the two matches of more than £100.

FRIENDLY REFUSAL

Public relations has not been a particularly strong point on many occasions as far as Exeter City Football Club are concerned. And it certainly was not the case in January 1970 when they greatly upset North Devon club Bideford. With Exeter having been knocked out of the FA Cup they had a blank Saturday fixture-wise, and so did Bideford, who suggested that City went to North Devon for a friendly. Exeter turned down their request saying that because of injury problems they had to decline their invitation.

Imagine then the Bideford club's disgust when three days later they read in the Press that Exeter City had agreed to play a friendly at Torquay United! Had those injuries miraculously cleared up? Or was it as suggested by some, that Exeter City did not fancy losing to Bideford? It was reported that the bad feeling caused by this lack of thought had prompted some North Devon supporters, who watched Bideford when City were away, to stay away altogether from St James's Park now.

GOALKEEPERS

Exeter City goalkeeper Jack Robinson, who played with the club during its first professional season in 1908, was something of a character both on and off the field. He was no friend of referees for he had a habit of disputing decisions.

On one occasion, after conceding a goal, Robinson walked out to the halfway line to protest to the referee, saying that a player had been offside. He was told to return to his goal by the official, but before he did, the charismatic goalkeeper promptly kicked the ball over the St James's Park Grandstand and out of the ground amid much laughter from the crowd. Surely he would have been sent off today, but then the referee decided a severe lecture was all that was needed.

Robinson also had the strange superstition of eating a rice pudding before games. This he said was to avoid the repetition of the occasion when he conceded eight goals at Sunderland!

Outfield players have on a number of occasions replaced goalkeepers for one reason or another whilst playing for Exeter City, but it is doubtful whether anyone will beat the record held by winger Charlie McClelland? He first took over the goalkeeper's shirt when Barney Singleton was injured in Exeter City's match at Bournemouth on Friday 23rd March 1951. The result was 1-1.

Just eight days later, Singleton was again injured at Norwich City, and McClelland stood in between the posts. Exeter lost 2-0. The following month, on 14th April, McClelland was called on yet again to keep goal, this time only for the final two minutes of the City Reserves game at home to Tonbridge, when Ken Salter was injured. City won 1-0. It didn't end there, as McClelland must have performed so well that he volunteered to play a complete game in goal after the Reserves were short of a 'keeper for their game at Merthyr Tydfil on 14th February 1953. Perhaps he was not as good as some thought, however, because City crashed to a 7-0 defeat!

Exeter City were so short of recognised forwards in April 1965 that goalkeeper Alan Barnett played centre-forward in their Western League match at Weston-super-Mare. City lost 3-1, but the scorer? Yes – Alan Barnett!

Goalkeeper Richard Smeath was pressed into service as one of the substitutes in Exeter City's match at Leyton Orient in October 1988. Defender Scott Hiley failed a late fitness test, and striker Jamie Harris was taken ill on the trip to London, leaving City with only eleven fit outfield players and two goalkeepers in the travelling party. Smeath who was not called upon, didn't make another first team league appearance for the club and was subsequently released.

Dave Walter became the first Exeter City goalkeeper to be sent off for the so called 'professional foul'. He was shown the red card in the game at St James's Park against Peterborough United in April 1989 after bringing down oncoming forward Nick Cusack. The incident occurred in the eighty fourth minute, defender Chris Banks took over between the posts and City won the match 3-1.

Exeter City have played a number of friendly games against local opposition over the years. This team photograph was taken before their game at Crediton in August 1954. Donning the goalkeeping jersey was winger Charlie McClelland, who played several games between the posts for the City, taking over from injured colleagues during a match, and being selected to play a whole 90 minutes as well. Back Row (L to R) Arnold Mitchell (with hair!), Fred Davey, Charlie McClelland, Dick Walton, Keith Harvey, Norman Douglass. Front Row (L to R) Gerry Priestley, John Anderson, Angus Mackay, Bill Ellaway, Maurice Setters.

Walter had signed for the City in November 1988 from Bideford and in doing so gave up his job as a foreman of a 1,300 acre estate in North Devon. He did, however, keep the land he owned at West Putford along with a large flock of breeding ewes.

The briefest goalkeeping appearance? That surely must be the unfortunate Blackburn Rovers goalkeeper Terry Gennoe who was stretchered off the field following a collision with Exeter City's Clive Whitehead after just seventy six seconds of the Littlewoods Cup tie at St James's Park in September 1989. Gennoe injured his neck and much concern was shown as Exeter City club doctor Robert Anderson administered treatment. An ambulance was backed into the St James's Road end and the player taken to hospital. Thankfully the injury was not as serious as first feared and Gennoe was able to rejoin his team-mates after the game, which ended in a 3-0 defeat for Blackburn.

Youth trainee goalkeeper Jamie Day made a substitute appearance in the Exeter City Reserves attack after only four minutes of their South West

Counties League fixture at Swansea City in November 1989. He replaced the injured Ben Rowe and went on to score one of the City goals in a 2-2 draw with the Welsh club.

Goalkeeper Steve Berryman who joined Exeter at the start of the 1990/91 season, was loaned to Exmouth Town for one game, whilst still on trial with the City. Exmouth were short of a keeper for their pre-season friendly against Plymouth Argyle. A week later Berryman signed a one year contract with Exeter City.

Berryman was selected as one of the substitutes for Exeter City's match at Bury in December 1990. He had been named as substitute as regular keeper Kevin Miller, although he played, was carrying an injury.

Berryman would have replaced Miller had the need arisen. Exeter lost 3-1, and Miller played the whole match.

GOALS

In a friendly fixture at Okehampton in November 1908, inside forward, Singlehurst, scored seven goals in Exeter City's 17-0 win.

Exeter City suffered something of a goal drought on their away travels during the 1923/24 season, to create an unwanted Football League record. They went fourteen away league fixtures without scoring. The dreadful run commenced on 23rd April 1923 when they lost 3-1 at Merthyr Tydfil. The next time City hit the back of the net came on 16th February 1924, as they won 1-0 at Swindon Town. During the 1923/24 Division Three South season, Exeter managed to score just a paltry four goals away from home.

Spectators were treated to fifteen goals in a friendly match played by the City against an Army XI at St James's Park on 14th January 1933. Exeter won by an amazing 10-5, with five goals being scored by Fred Whitlow.

This is an early 1970s photo with Alan Banks looking on as Joe Gadston launches himself in a bid to score at St James's Park.

Twelve months later the goals flowed again – seventeen this time! A Third Division South Cup tie against Crystal Palace on Wednesday 24th January 1934 ended in an incredible 11-6 win for Exeter. Ace scorer Fred Whitlow again did the damage with a personal tally of six goals.

When Exeter City defeated Aldershot 8-1 at St James's Park on 8th May 1935 in a Third Division South match, all the goals were scored in the second half.

Similarly, and more recently in April 1986, it was 0-0 at half-time in the Macbar Midweek League fixture between Cardiff City Reserves and Exeter City Reserves. Exeter's goal machine then clicked with a vengeance as they ran in nine second-half goals without reply.

Stan Hurst scored eight goals in Exeter City Reserves' 14-0 victory over St Luke's College in an Exeter and District League fixture at St James's Park on Wednesday 9th October 1935. The half-time score was 9-0 in City's favour, five of the goals having been scored by Hurst.

Ray Carter scored after just ten seconds in the home match against Accrington Stanley on 21st October 1961. City went on to win 3-0, while the Accrington club went into liquidation the following March with debts of £60,000.

Winger Roger Smith gave himself an early present as he scored two goals, his first for the club, in Exeter City's 3-2 home win over Halifax Town in October 1966. Smith, who had been signed from Tottenham Hotspur during the close season, travelled back to London after the game for an important appointment. The following day he got married!

Saturday, Nov. 19th, 1960
Fourth Division

EXETER CITY
VERSUS
ACCRINGTON S.
Kick-off 3 p.m.

Official Programme 4D

GRECIANS ASSOCIATION

The Grecians Association were formed in 1945 – but for their successful fund raising activities over a number of years, there is little doubt that Exeter City Football Club would have been in even more serious financial difficulties on several occasions.

At the first meeting in 1945, eight ardent Exeter City supporters each donated five shillings to the fund to start the Grecians Association. The aim of the Association was to assist the Football Club in any way it could, either financially or from a practical point of view.

In the first twenty years of the Grecians Association's existence nearly £25,000 was handed over to the parent club – Exeter City. They also made generous contributions towards new floodlights, a fully equipped medical room, dressing room renovations, and ground improvements in general, including the Norman Kendall and Grecians Gates.

All manner of fund raising events were held, including the weekly Red and White Club draw which eventually, when established, became a separate organisation. Bingo, dances, jackpot competitions, and various draws have all contributed towards keeping professional football at St James's Park.

An Exmouth branch of the Exeter City Grecians Association was formed in January 1948 with team manager George Roughton attending the inaugural meeting. By the following September it was reported that the branch had recruited ninety members. The Exmouth branch chairman Mr Hallett estimated that five hundred fans were travelling regularly from the Exmouth area to City home fixtures.

Before the start of Exeter City's match with Aldershot in October 1955, a new set of nets were formally handed over to the club by the Exmouth branch of the Grecians Association. Master Mervyn Scoble shot into an empty net at the Big Bank end watched by the City team to christen the new nets.

The Grecians Association ceased to function as from 1st July 1970, following a merger with the Exeter City Supporters Club. The new title was 'The Exeter City Supporters Club (The Grecians)'. The Exeter City Supporters Club had been formed following promotion to the Third Division in 1964, but it was felt by all concerned that a merged organisation would be beneficial to the parent club – Exeter City F.C.

Trouble lay ahead for the newly merged group however. For in June 1971, nineteen of the twenty five committee members resigned, and the new Exeter City Supporters Club folded. A new association was to be formed to include Commercial Manager John Hillier, and his assistant. The Exeter City Board of Directors issued a statement to the effect that everyone had parted on the best of terms and that there had been no disagreement.

The statement issued was however not quite true, for it was widely known that the Supporters Club Committee felt that they served no useful purpose as there was now a full time Commercial Manager, who was about to be joined by an assistant. This was perhaps further confirmed by City director, Wally Rice, who added that it was now the intention of his fellow directors that all fund raising activities should be administered entirely by Exeter City Football Club.

To further add fuel to the argument that all had not been well between the Exeter City Supporters Club (The Grecians) and the parent club, a few weeks later a new organisation known as the 'Grecians Sports and Charities Association' was formed by some of the committee who had resigned. Their aim was to continue with the weekly bingo sessions, with the profits not as before going to Exeter City Football Club, but in future to deserving causes in the City of Exeter. To prove their point, a £50 cheque was presented to the Exeter St Thomas Senior Citizens Club by the new Grecians group President, Mr Percy Hilton.

Meanwhile yet another supporters group was formed by Exeter City Football Club known as the 'Exeter City Supporters Association'. Their aim was to raise funds for the football club by adopting a professional approach. The Exeter City Football Club was to have control of the new Association finances.

GROUND SAFETY

Following the tragic Bradford City Football Club fire on 11th May 1985, a number of safety requirements became compulsory at all grounds including St James's Park. In 1985 Exeter City had to apply for a Ground Safety Certificate from the Exeter City Council. A Government Inspector surveyed the Park and reported back with a number of essential conditions which had to be met by the club.

The main Grandstand was a particular problem. Exits and seating modifications had to be made, whilst the complete structure had to be fireproofed. Naturally, this involved expenditure of several thousands of pounds which the club could ill afford. The strict safety conditions had to be complied with, and a grant was available from the Football Grounds Improvement Trust. The club could apply for a grant to meet 75 per cent of the total cost of the work involved. However, City had to foot the bills themselves first and then reclaim the money from the Trust!

The Grandstand would have had to have remained closed if the work had not been carried out. The stand, constructed almost entirely of wood, was an area of real concern, and a series of meetings was held between the club, local Fire Brigade and Police officers. One of the conditions was that the Grandstand needed to be cleared in three and a half minutes should the outbreak of fire occur. Exits from the stand would therefore have to be reviewed, including access being gained from the front of the stand onto the pitch.

The Exeter City Board of Directors approached the City Council for possible financial assistance, but this was refused as they had already been lent £60,000 interest free, which was in the process of being repaid. With the commencement of the 1985/86 season just three days away, the club were told that the capacity of St James's Park would be cut to just 7,050, later raised to 8,569, until certain safety works had been satisfactorily undertaken. The Cowshed was put totally out of bounds while work went ahead on the terracing, safety barriers, and exits. The Cowshed usually held a maximum of 4,500 spectators. A compromise was reached, however, and up to 1,500 spectators were allowed to take their places in the Cowshed area. At the same time the capacity of the Grandstand was reduced from 1,700 to 1,300. This was achieved by closing the back four rows of seats and widening the gangways by removing further seats.

The Big Bank end did not escape either, with the capacity being reduced from 7,500 to 4,800. This would remain in force until crash barriers had been improved, and gates from the terracing fitted to swing outwards rather than inwards. The visitors' end had its capacity cut from 2,500 to 950 for the same reasons.

Exeter City chairman Byron Snell estimated that all the work to comply with all the ground safety conditions would cost £750,000. The immediate task was to completely refurbish the Cowshed, including new terracing, barriers, and roofing, at a total cost of between £150,000 and £200,000.

In October 1985 Exeter City were further instructed by the police to provide a one metre walkway for their officers at the front of the Cowshed. The new fence would cost £7,000. Work on the Cowshed area went on for at least twelve months, finally being completed in October 1986. The refurbished Cowshed area was officially re-opened by the then England team manager Bobby Robson prior to the Fourth Division match with Southend United.

No sooner had City met one safety requirement then another appeared to be needed either by the fire, police, ambulance service, or the city council. From the supporters' point of view, and no doubt the club's, it seemed frustrating that a concerted plan of action had not been drawn up in the first place instead of apparent piecemeal alterations which only pushed the final cost up when the club could not really afford it. Safety of spectators was of course paramount in everyone's eyes, but planning of improvements did seem a little haphazard.

In 1989 Lord Justice Taylor's report into safety at Football Grounds following the Hillsborough disaster, when ninety five Liverpool fans were crushed to death, led to further measures being taken at St James's Park. After consultations with the various services, the Devon County Safety and Ground Licensing Committee recommended along with other points, that the Well Street exit from the Big Bank had to be widened, and gangways marked out on the terracing from top to bottom.

Work on replacing all the crush barriers on the Big Bank took place during

the 1990 close season. Exeter also submitted plans to meet safety requirements in the Grandstand which were given the go ahead by Devon County Council's Safety Committee.

In the close season of 1991, still the safety improvements went on. The steep steps from the rear of the Grandstand were demolished and rebuilt. New exit gates were fitted to the terracing areas, and a new fence constructed alongside the railway embankment at the Well Street entrance. New facilities were provided for the Police and the St John Ambulance Brigade at the top of the Big Bank.

GROUNDS

When Exeter City arrived at Torquay United's Cricketfield ground, situated just off the sea front, for a friendly fixture in February 1905, they found that the playing area was anything but full size. The centre of the field was roped off where the cricket squares were situated. The football pitch was marked out towards one side, but this meant that the width of the pitch was some twenty yards shorter than the minimum regulation. In consequence the ball frequently went out of play and there was little room for passing movements of any note. There were plenty of goals scored though with Exeter City winning 6-3!

Exeter City were the first ever club to play at The Valley in August 1921, home of Charlton Athletic. A 9,000 crowd saw Charlton win with the only goal of the game scored by Tommy Dowling.

Exeter were also one of only thirteen clubs to play Charlton Athletic at their Catford ground. Charlton had moved to Catford from The Valley for the 1923/24 season, but it proved to be a disastrous venture and they quickly returned to their original home.

City actually played at Catford twice! On the first occasion the match was abandoned after fifty minutes with the score standing at 1-1, and Wilf Livesley scoring for the Grecians. The abandonment followed torrential rain which left the surface waterlogged. In the re-arranged match later in the season Charlton won 1-0.

Aldershot's ground is situated in a public park, and back in April 1933 when Exeter City visited it, the facilities were still pretty basic with little covered accommodation. Five thousand spectators saw the Shots win 4-1, but part of the terracing consisted of army Kit Boxes and benches on which some of the crowd stood!

Exeter City Reserves played a friendly match at Dawlish to mark the official opening of that club's new ground on Wednesday 11th September 1935. City won 2-1 before an attendance estimated to be around 1,000.

Heavitree United's ground was used by the City players for training sessions in July 1954. This was because the St James's Park pitch had been re-seeded and was not ready to be used without damaging the surface.

John Newman

In August 1973, John Newman, the Exeter City manager, performed the opening ceremony at Ottery St Mary Football Club, to mark the completion of new dressing rooms at the Washbrook Meadows ground. The Exeter first team then played a friendly fixture with the Otters, winning 2-0, both the City goals being scored by Alan Devlin.

John Newman and the Exeter City team performed a similar task twelve months later at Tavistock Football Club. After opening the new dressing rooms at Langford Park the City defeated Tavistock 3-1 with two goals from Lammie Robertson and one from Nicky Jennings. Off target shooting at one end meant that watching cows were occasionally hit!

GROUNDSMEN

The longest serving groundsman at Exeter City was Sonny Clarke who joined the club in 1953, and finally retired through ill health over thirty years later. He is regarded as being one of the best, if not the best groundsman the club has ever had. Sonny was so highly thought of that his long service and dedication was rewarded with a benefit match against Derby County in October 1980. Sonny turned his talents to wine making following his retirement as groundsman and won a cup in a competition with the Exeter and District Wine Circle.

HOLY MATTERS

The goalscoring Reverend! The Reverend Reid joined Exeter City in 1904, having previously played

Sonny Clarke

for Swindon Town and he soon showed his goalscoring prowess. He became the first City player to score a hat-trick in a league match during a 3-1 home win over St Luke's College in October 1904. His goalscoring form led him to be selected for the Devon County team on several occasions.

The Reverend Reid made contact with his former club in December 1949. He was granted permission by the Exeter City Board of Directors to launch an appeal in the match programme for the third round FA Cup-tie against Chester. The appeal read: "The Exeter City Board of Directors have generously granted me permission to have a collection on the ground towards the restoration fund of my old church, St Mary Arches. The church was badly damaged and made unusable in the 1942 blitz, but we hope to have it restored sufficiently to use again at Easter."

A Vicar from Topsham, the Reverend R. Knight, was on Exeter City's books during the 1911/12 season. He was also a Devon County cricketer. Whilst he never made the City first team, he made many appearances for the Reserves.

The Bishop of Exeter attended Exeter City's 2-2 draw against Wrexham in October 1967. He took his place on the Big Bank for the first half, before retiring to the directors' box for the second forty five minutes.

The Exeter Cathedral Schoolboys' football team was coached by Exeter City winger Barry Rowan during the 1971/72 season.

Exeter City appointed their first official club chaplain, 29-year-old Richard Chewter, in March 1984. Having moved to Exeter four years earlier he had become a keen City supporter. He said, "I do not pray for goals, I pray for souls. The Chaplain is the guy who represents God in the Football Club."

Theo Foley, the genial Irishman who played full back for Exeter City between 1955 and 1961, and who later was involved with the management of Northampton, Millwall and Arsenal, took over the coaching of the St Nicholas School team from a nun, Sister Marie Alfred.

HOSTILITIES

Exeter City players were among those who lost their lives during the First World War. Arthur Evans was killed in the first battle of the Somme. Reserve team players Clarke, Augustus Harding, Fred Hunt and Kadie White were also killed in the hostilities. In addition, Fred Marshall, badly wounded, Fred Goodwin, and Herbert Tierney, who lost the sight of his right eye, were to take no further part in the game because of their injuries.

Half back William Smith sadly had to have a leg amputated, in a Liverpool hospital in 1919, as a result of injuries received. A collection for the unfortunate Smith was taken before the start of City's game with Northampton Town in November 1919. The Exeter Military Band under the conductorship of Mr George Newman also sacrificed their usual collection in the interests of Smith. The collection raised £33.

Former Exeter City player, Joe Bulcock, who played for the club in the 1908/09 season, was another to perish in the hostilities.

At the invitation of the Exeter City Board of Directors, several soldiers who had been wounded in the early encounters of the First World War took their places in the Grandstand for the Southern League game against Millwall in November 1914. Among those present was former City amateur player, Sergeant Hyde of the Devon Regiment, who had played one first team match in each of the 1906/07, and 1907/08 seasons.

Forward Charlie Vowles, signed by Exeter City in 1920, spent five years in India serving with the 21st Lancers, and took part in the last cavalry charge made by the British Army. Whilst in India he played in the All India Shield match.

The last Football League fixture that Exeter City played before the competition was suspended for the duration of the Second World War, was at Port Vale on Saturday 2nd September 1939. Harold Riley scored the only goal to give City the points and put them into second place in the table. On the same afternoon at St James's Park, the City Reserves drew 0-0 with Hereford United in a Southern League encounter, again the last to be played until the cessation of hostilities.

With many American Servicemen being stationed in the area, a game of American Football between the Sea Lions and McKees Maulers was staged at St James's Park on Sunday 7th January 1945 in aid of the Merchant Navy Comforts Fund.

The Maulers were 'mauled' by 13 points to 6. Before the game the ceremony of trooping the United States flag took place with the Devonshire Regimental Band being in attendance. The European Baseball Championship Final was also staged at the Park on 23rd August 1945. The American Army from France outclassed and defeated the United States Navy, Exeter by ten runs to nil in front of a crowd of 1,500.

Players guesting for clubs was a common practice during the Second World War. Exeter City inside forward George Wardle had the distinction of playing at Wembley for the Chelsea side that defeated Millwall in the 1945 Football League South Cup Final.

Exeter City chairman, Captain Hunter, was among the casualties during the blitz of Exeter in 1942. He died from injuries received. Twenty-year-old Goalkeeper Ken Halliday, who had been recommended to Exeter City by former player Reg Clarke, and signed amateur forms, lost his life in a training accident with the R.A.F. in May 1945.

A number of friendly matches were played at St James's Park during 1945 in aid of various fund raising organisations. These included Exeter City against a Royal Marines side for The Royal Marines Prisoner of War Fund. The Great Western Railway played a Southern Railway team in aid of the Red Cross Prisoner of War Fund.

Exeter also travelled to Weymouth where they played The Devonshire Regiment in aid of Merchant Navy Week.

INJURIES

The unluckiest triallist at Exeter City has to be inside forward Stanley Welsh, a young amateur from the Southampton area. He was given a trial by the City in a Plymouth and District League match at St James's Park against

The Royal Marines in February 1910. After scoring the opening goal of the game, Welsh was carried off the field with a broken leg following a collision with an opposing player. The Marines won the match 2-1.

INLAND REVENUE

Exeter City successfully appealed against a rates increase in 1955 imposed by the Inland Revenue after the Grandstand roof had been repainted! Rates were to be raised from the original figure of £234, agreed in 1935, to £247. The Inland Revenue proposed the increase because of an advertisement which appeared on the Grandstand roof. Following an appeal, however, the increase was rejected by the valuation panel for Exeter, East and North Devon. In Exeter City's defence, it was stated by the club solicitor Mr J. Scott that no rent was payable to the club for the advertisement. In 1952 the roof of the Grandstand was in a bad state and the club could not afford the £300 to have it repainted. However a keen supporter of the club agreed to repaint it if his company could advertise on the roof in return – the company being Regent Oil.

JUST VISITING

A day visit with a difference? Exeter City defender Ellis Crompton had transferred to Bristol Rovers during the summer of 1913. He returned however in August of that year to watch his former City team-mates play a pre-season practice match. Two Exeter sides took to the field for a game between the Probables and the Possibles. In the second half, the watching and popular Ellis was invited to take over as linesman from a Mr H. Ford. He happily accepted, with the Possibles winning 3-0.

Crompton actually enjoyed a long second spell with Exeter City as a player when he rejoined the club in 1921 going on to make 145 league appearances.

KIT

Until November 1910, Exeter City played in a green and white kit. The players however petitioned the Board of Directors that the colours were bringing them no luck at all. The directors decided that as from the home match against West Ham United on 12th November 1910, the team would wear red and white striped shirts, and white shorts. At the same time as dispensing with the 'unlucky' green and white kit, the band who welcomed the City team onto the pitch at every home game to the sound of 'Uncle Tom Cobley', decided to stop playing the famous Devonian tune as well.

For the visit of Southampton to St James's Park in December 1913, the City team completely changed their kit to avoid clashing with the red and white striped shirts worn by the visitors. They wore chocolate shirts with yellow sleeves!

A pre-season practice match in 1919 played between two Exeter City

EXETER CITY F.C. 1911-12

E. WHITTAKER, H. EVANS, J. RUTTER, A. COATES, W. WHITTAKER, F. PRIDEAUX, F. CORNAN, C. PRATT, J. BANKS (TRAINER), G. PARNELL, S. BASSETT, MR. J. H. THOMAS, MR. A. CHADWICK, R. WATSON, T. GRIFFITHS, J. GAR... (SECRETARY) (MANAGER) H. LOCKETT. J. FORT. CADDIE

teams saw one of the sides take to the field in the usual red and white stripes, while the other City team played in crimson and amber. The same crimson and amber combination was worn by City's first team for their home match against Southampton in January 1920.

Exeter City wore red and white hooped shirts for the first time for their opening game of the 1946/47 season against Torquay United at St James's Park. It had proved impossible to buy the more usual City shirts of vertical stripes. At one stage it was rumoured that the team might have to wear a one plain colour shirt or even squares!

In August 1947 Exeter City appealed to supporters to donate their unwanted clothing coupons to assist with the purchase of shirts, shorts and stockings. Whilst a certain allocation of clothing coupons were made available to clubs by the Football Association through the Board of Trade, it was not enough to fully kit out two teams. An arrangement existed with the Board of Trade whereby any coupons donated from supporters were exchanged for vouchers.

In the same month a practice match was played behind closed doors at the Park between two teams of City players. One team wore shirts, the other played in their 'skins'. They were described as, "gleaming like bronzed Gods" in the streaming summer sunshine.

The red and white hooped shirts were dispensed with for the 1950/51 season, with Exeter then wearing red shirts and white shorts.

For their FA Cup tie at Brentford in November 1958, Exeter City bought a brand new playing strip so as not to clash with the red and white of the home side. They played in tangerine shirts with black edgings, white shorts, and white socks.

The start of Exeter City's Western League match at Minehead in March 1966 was delayed after the home side discovered that their shirts had not been brought to the ground. Eventually a set was obtained, but the wait seemed to affect the City more than Minehead as they lost 2-0.

For the 1966/67 season Exeter changed their colours from a predominant red to a rather uninspiring all white strip with red trimmings. This was not met with much supporters' approval however and the traditional red and white striped shirts were re-introduced for the 1968/69 season. The change colours for 1968/69 was blue and white stripes.

They have continued to wear red and white striped shirts ever since, apart from the 1977/78 season when the all white strip briefly returned, and for a time in the 1980s an all red kit was worn. The change kit during the 1988/89 season was sky blue shirts with navy shorts and socks.

Exeter City trainer Jimmy Gallagher was forced to play in an FA Cup tie at Grimsby Town in January 1949 when several players went down with food poisoning the day before the match. Gallagher is seen in this team group of the 1949/50 squad of players. Back Row (L to R) Cyril Johnstone, Fred Davey, Ray Goddard, Ken Powell, Bernard 'Barney' Singleton, Bill Harrower, Jim Clark, Steve Walker, Jimmy Gallagher (trainer). Front Row (L to R) Peter Fallon, Dick Smart, Archie Smith, John Greenwood, Dougie Regan.

52

A rather uninspiring all white kit, with red flashes, was re-introduced for the 1977/78 season. The Exeter City team are shown at the pre-season photo-call. Back Row (L to R) Keith Ford, Keith Bowker, Harry Holman, Bobby Saxton (player-manager). Middle Row (L to R) Lammie Robertson, John Templeman, John Baugh, Richard Key, Phil Howe, Bobby Hodge, Peter Hatch. Front row (L to R) Jack Edwards (trainer), Nicky Jennings, Graham Weeks, Johnny Hore, Tony Kellow, Alan Beer, Tony Long (physio). Seated on ground Paul Smythe, Roy Ireland.

LEAGUELINER

For the 1972/73 season the Football League chartered a train which was available for hire at £1,000 by clubs for transporting supporters to away fixtures. It was a train with a difference, however, with the carriages being converted into a discotheque, cinema, etc. Exeter City hired the train for their fixture at Peterborough United in April 1973.

At just £3.50 per head, 336 supporters made the trip. Manager John Newman and the players also made the journey on the train in a reserved coach. The day was a big success, City drew the match 1-1, and the club made a profit on the train of around £300.

It was not a success for the coachload of supporters from Ilfracombe though. They missed the train at the arranged pick-up point of Taunton railway station, their journey taking longer than expected across from North Devon!

Various competitions were held for the supporters throughout the train journey including a draw for which the truly riveting prize of an Exeter City garden pixie was on offer! On the return journey, a few of the players visited the 'disco' coach, and Fred Binney even gave an impromptu playing and singing session on the keyboards.

The only complaints received on the day concerned the refreshments which ran out! No fewer than 1,800 cans of beer were consumed, and among the items eaten by the hungry supporters were 200 pasties, 100 chicken pieces, 100 oranges, and 200 bananas!

LEYLAND DAF CUP

Torquay United's secretary angered Exeter City officials following his remarks that Exeter had fielded an under strength team against Bristol Rovers in the Leyland Daf Cup in January 1990. Torquay, Bristol Rovers and Exeter City were in the same group in the competition, and two of the three clubs qualified for the next round. Torquay were upset that Exeter allegedly fielded an under strength team, for had City beaten Bristol Rovers, instead of losing 3-0, Torquay and not Rovers would have progressed to the next round along with Exeter. Torquay requested that the Football League investigate the matter.

The Football League asked Exeter City to furnish them with medical evidence that certain players had not been fit to play at Bristol Rovers. A month later Exeter were completely cleared of the allegations when a Football League commission of enquiry held in Bristol dismissed Torquay's claims.

The commission consisted of League Secretary David Dent, President and Blackburn Rovers chairman Bill Fox, and Aston Villa chairman Doug Ellis. They interviewed both Exeter City manager Terry Cooper, and club doctor Robert Anderson. They were satisfied that City fielded their strongest possible team available and no further action was taken.

The commission had also summoned to the enquiry six of the Exeter players who had missed the game at Bristol Rovers, but they were not after all asked to give evidence. The six involved were Danny Bailey (he actually played as substitute but was not fully fit), Kevin Miller, Steve Neville, Darren Rowbotham, Shaun Taylor and Clive Whitehead.

The Exeter City team that had faced Bristol Rovers and upset Torquay United: Dave Walter, Scott Hiley, Ian Benjamin, Jim McNichol, Herbie Heath, Mark Cooper, Paul Eshelby, Paul Batty, Phil Lock, Brian McDermott, Tony Frankland. Substitutes – Danny Bailey and Lee Annunziata.

LIMITED COMPANY

The Exeter City Board of Directors announced a plan to form a new £100,000 Limited Company in December 1964. A special meeting of shareholders was held at the Rougemont Hotel the following month to discuss the idea. The aim of the new company was to put the club on a firmer financial footing and to make further progress.

The new company, was to be known as Properties (Exeter) Limited. It would assume all the responsibilities of the Exeter City Football and Athletic Company Limited, and Exeter Residential Properties Limited (this had been formed to administer the players' club houses).

An important provision would have to be agreed before the new company was formed. This was to involve the new company giving a lease to the Football Club in perpetuity for as long as professional soccer under the auspices of the Football League and the Football Association continued to be played at St James's Park.

Club chairman Reg Rose reminded shareholders that the current amount of indebtedness was very substantial. The objectives of the new company would be to relieve the club of the liability of the then £7,000 mortgage and of the directors' loans amounting to £14,000. These would be transferred to the new company as part of the share capital. The company would assume responsibility for the building society mortgages on the existing club houses and would relieve the club of all financial guarantees. In return for the company taking over the expenditure and liabilities it was suggested that St James's Park should be transferred to the company along with the club houses, the football club being issued with shares in the new company. At the same time Properties (Exeter) Limited would protect the club by guaranteeing to it the lease on the St James's Park ground.

Mr Rose told shareholders that "only a bunch of idiots" would do what his fellow directors proposed to do to help the club. He put forward the resolution to form the new company and this was passed by 6,114 votes to 2,077. All properties and liabilities of Exeter City would therefore be transferred to Properties (Exeter) Limited.

It was interesting to note that of those 6,114 votes in favour, each vote representing one share in Exeter City Football Club, no fewer than 4,747 were held by the Board of Directors! Mr Rose held 2,078 shares, and Messrs Cowley (750), Dart (565), Gillin (750), and Rodgers (601). Up to and including December 1964 a total of 19,755 shares had been issued, although it was widely thought that many had probably been lost, forgotten about, or just thrown away.

Mr Rose added that at that time money in the club was on loan and that each director could recall the loan at six month's notice. By forming the new company each director would agree that his money was in the company for good. Directors could sell their stake, however, only if someone was willing to buy them out. Mr Rose gave an assurance that the new company would mean more money for the Football Club. It had been in the interests of Exeter City Football Club, and not the directors that the resolution had been passed.

MANAGERS

Arthur Chadwick, Exeter City's first manager in 1908 until leaving the club in December 1922 for Reading, sadly collapsed and died in the Grandstand at St James's Park in March 1936 when paying a return visit to watch his former club play Clapton Orient.

No fewer than three North Devon clubs were managed by former Exeter City players during the 1953/54 season. Harry Bartholomew was in charge at Ilfracombe Town, whilst Arthur Coles was Barnstaple Town's manager. They were joined towards the end of the season by Ray Goddard who took over at Bideford as player-manager.

Bill Thompson, who had a short spell as Exeter City manager between May 1957 and January 1958 was once quoted as saying, "I believe the manager has no place and no right to be on the touchline." He nearly always watched games from the directors' box.

Which Exeter City manager was appointed in a corridor underneath the Grandstand at Southampton? Answer – Frank Broome. He was Bill Thompson's successor in 1958, and had just watched Exeter lose 6-0 to the Saints, although Mr Broome had actually missed the first four goals due to the late arrival of his train! City chairman Albert Line had a ten minute chat with

Broome in the corridor, called over two of his fellow directors, and then shortly after announced the appointment of Exeter City's new manager.

Frank Broome returned for a second spell as manager in April 1967, and once again the circumstances in which he accepted the post was a little unusual. He was in Australia when the City chairman Les Kerslake spoke to Mr Broome offering him the position. Within days Mr Kerslake received a cable back which read: "Accept position at terms stated."

It was some three weeks before Mr Broome arrived in Exeter from Australia where he had been successfully coaching a Sydney-based club. He did however manage to watch City's final match of the 1966/67 season, which resulted in a 1-0 win over Notts County before facing a busy close season re-building his playing squad.

When Cyril Spiers left by mutual consent as manager of Exeter City in February 1962, it could not have been because of a recent poor set of results! The team had not played for six weeks due the arctic grip the weather had on most of the country. It therefore appeared to be extremely strange timing when the Board of Directors announced that Mr Spiers was to leave the club.

Team manager Jack Edwards was severely censured by the Football Association following a report received by them from the match referee in charge of Exeter City's game with Darlington in October 1963. He was warned as to his future conduct and ordered to give a written undertaking to the FA that the reported incidents would not recur in the future.

It is a well known fact in football that when the manager of a team receives a vote of confidence in his ability from the Board of Directors, then the sack is not that far away! So perhaps it really was no surprise that after the Exeter City chairman gave his support to manager Jim Iley that he was on his way out of St James's Park a few months later. The chairman, Byron Snell, in January 1985 was quoted as saying, "In Jim Iley we have got a first class manager, who is prepared to stick to his task. He has got the full support of the Board." Just over three months later Iley was sacked!

The dismissal of Iley caused an uproar among the club's supporters, and the former manager took the unusual step of calling a public meeting to put his side of the story and relate various events that had taken place during his spell at the Park much to the embarrassment and anger of the Board of Directors. The meeting which attracted around 150 people took place in the Sidwell Street Methodist Church Hall.

Iley later took Exeter City to the County Court to press for damages for wrongful dismissal. After an initial appearance, and approaching the club to settle out of court, the long running 'saga' finally came to a conclusion when Iley announced in February 1986 that an amicable settlement had indeed been reached between himself and Exeter City.

Ironically, when Jim Iley had visited St James's Park as Player-manager of Peterborough United in December 1969, he had severely, and quite rightly, criticised certain sections of the Exeter City supporters when they chanted 'Get him off' at injured player Eddie Holliday. The unfortunate winger had broken a leg, and it took several minutes before the player was carried off on a stretcher. Iley who was disgusted with the reaction of some of the supporters said: "The crowd showed a lack of tolerance, heart, and understanding during the delay."

Two of the Peterborough players went over to a section of the crowd who were chanting to show their disgust at the impatience shown by them, and Jim Iley exchanged angry words with supporters in the Grandstand.

Jim Iley's successor, caretaker-manager and former player John Hore, also left the club a bitter man. He claimed he had been promised the manager's job by the Exeter City chairman but was overlooked in favour of the appointment of Colin Appleton. Hore said he had been: "led up the garden path. I cannot accept the way in which the chairman and the Board have conducted themselves in this matter."

John Hore

Exeter City manager Terry Cooper was enraged at a tackle on Scott Hiley by a Lincoln City player at St James's Park in November 1989. The Lincoln man was ordered off the field, but the tackle prompted Cooper to leap from the dug-out to show his anger. The Lincoln City manager Colin Murphy stood and stared long and hard at Cooper before the referee intervened to calm down the situation. Police presence was called for, and the two managers returned to their dug-outs. Exeter won the game 3-0.

Terry Cooper took the unusual step of joining the loyal travelling band of Exeter City supporters on the terraces at Hartlepool after their side had gone 2-0 down in the second half of the game in November 1988. Cooper was annoyed at the way the City had been playing and felt that the supporters deserved a word of praise for their efforts in travelling all the way to Hartlepool, only to see a poor Exeter City performance. With Cooper chatting to the supporters an amazing transformation took place, with City scoring twice in the last four minutes through Darren Rowbotham and Shaun Taylor to make the final score 2-2!

MASCOTS and LUCKY CHARMS

The club adopted what they hoped would be a lucky black cat in August 1921. A starving stray kitten strolled into St James's Park and scratched at the office door. The cat was duly fed and enjoyed a bowl of milk before settling down to sleep. The staff adopted the cat and looked after it for the rest of the season as an unofficial mascot. Although the cat was reported to have taken a great interest in the players' training it did not really prove to be lucky, as the City ended the 1921/22 season next to bottom in the Third Division South.

Prior to Exeter City's second round FA Cup tie at St James's Park against Aston Villa in January 1914, a 'lucky mascot' was led through the streets of Exeter! The mascot? – A goat! The animal wearing red and white favours was purchased by a group of Exeter taxi drivers to be presented to City team captain Jimmy Rigby. One wonders what happened to this 'lucky' animal, for City lost 2-1!

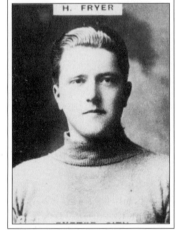

H. FRYER

Goalkeeper Harry Fryer was given a mascot of a different kind prior to the kick-off at Seaton Town, where Exeter City were engaged in a friendly fixture. Harry was presented with a monkey wearing a red ribbon. The monkey was tied up at the back of his goalnet. Fryer, nicknamed 'Tarzan', spent two seasons with Exeter after signing from Luton Clarence in 1921.

Hedley Boyce first followed Exeter City in the 1920s and continued to do so until his death in the 1980s. The 'pint sized' supporter was well known character around St James's Park, among fellow supporters, players and directors. He spent one season as the official Exeter City club mascot, and ran around the pitch at home matches, suitably attired in City colours, whipping up the crowd's enthusiasm upon the entry of their 'heroes'. Hedley was also at one time a programme seller outside the ground. He could often be seen walking around the city centre during the middle of the week, still attired in a red and white scarf and bobble hat. Exeter City Football Club was his life.

Hedley was forced to retire as the club mascot in November 1964, when he was off work for several weeks after badly straining a leg muscle. He decided to make way for a younger man, as he was aged 54! His place was taken by a much younger person – the 6-year-old son of Exeter City

Supporters Club committee man, Percy Whitcombe.

Mr Boyce was admitted to hospital in December 1968, after escaping from a house fire with eleven other people in Church Road, St Thomas. He soon recovered, however, as City manager Frank Broome visited him in hospital and news came through that Exeter had been drawn at home to Manchester United in the FA Cup

Another character, but not so much a mascot, was Gilbert Whyte. He first supported the City in 1949, travelling from his Okehampton home. A football fan through and through he could often be seen standing on the terraces at Torquay United and Plymouth Argyle, when his beloved Exeter City were away from home. He also followed the fortunes of both the Exeter Falcons Speedway team and Exeter Cricket Club.

Gilbert helped around St James's Park for a number of years with all manner of tasks, particularly assisting groundsman Sonny Clarke to prepare the playing surface. He could always be seen standing on the St James's Park terraces holding a transistor radio against his ear, when he would relay all the latest scores from other matches to the City supporters stood around him.

Gilbert died in October 1985, and such had been his popularity over the years that many of the City staff attended his funeral to pay their last respects.

Fulham supporter Pamela Leng brought her lucky black cat and mascot along to St James's Park for the Londoners' FA Cup tie against Exeter City in November 1969. The cat, three and a half months old, was called Saint Jiffrindale, the cup-tie being the twelfth match he had attended along with Miss Leng. Neither owner, or cat, could have been too impressed with Fulham, however, as they were sent crashing out of the Cup with City winning 2-0.

Former Exeter City odd job man Fred Camp was given a horseshoe by a farmer, and he, along with Exeter City groundsman Colin Wheatcroft, in July 1989 decided to nail it over the home dressing room door. The horseshoe was going to be painted red, but the farmer insisted that it would lose its lucky charm if they did that. City then proceeded to go 31 home matches without defeat and won the Fourth Division Championship. Only then did Colin Wheatcroft mention Exeter's lucky horseshoe as he had not wanted to tempt fate!

MATCHES

The visit of Torquay United to St James's Park in March 1907 proved to be something of a farce. The Torquay team did not turn up at the ground until 4.20 p.m. by which time several of Exeter City Reserves team had already gone home assuming that the match was not going to take place. Exeter, however, managed to field a scratch team, but not surprisingly lost the East Devon League fixture 4-1.

The Exeter City first and reserve teams both played matches on the same day at St James's Park on Easter Monday 1910. The Reserves won the first game 2-0, a Plymouth and District League fixture, against Woodland Villa. This was followed by a Southern League match which City lost 1-0 to Brighton and Hove Albion.

Similarly two matches were played on the same day at Home Park by City and the Reserves. On the afternoon of Wednesday 29th April 1914, the Reserves lost 2-1 to the Fourth Middlesex Regiment in a Plymouth and District League fixture. This was followed by the Spooner Cup match between Plymouth Argyle and Exeter City which was won by the Grecians 1-0.

Exeter's Southern League fixture at Portsmouth in November 1913 kicked off earlier than usual so that the referee, Mr Heath, could catch a railway connection back to his Birmingham home after the game!

The 1930/31 season opened in heatwave conditions. Exeter City entertained Norwich City at St James's Park on August 30th, and such was the heat that buckets of water were

A 1937 practice match at St James's Park with square goal posts and no nets?

strategically placed around the ground by the St John Ambulancemen as they treated at least two spectators who had been overcome by the conditions. A crowd of 6,000 saw Percy Varco score the only goal of the match to give Exeter the points.

Hundreds of Exeter supporters gathered outside the *Express and Echo* newspaper offices for news of their team's match at Sunderland in the quarter-final of the F.A. Cup in 1931. A mighty cheer arose when it was announced that City had drawn, and were bringing Sunderland back for a replay. When the newspaper seller appeared with copies of the *Football Express* edition of the newspaper, he was besieged by supporters all eager to buy copies and read of how their heroes had achieved such a marvellous result.

The all Devon final of the 1934 Third Division South Cup Final between

Exeter City and Torquay United was played at Home Park, Plymouth, in front of 6,198 spectators. City won the game 1-0, with a second half goal from Crediton-born Stan Hurst. At the end of the game the cup was presented to City's captain, Reg Clarke, by the Chairman of Crystal Palace Football Club Louis Bellattie.

Exeter City took part in a benefit match for the Plymouth Albion Rugby Union Club on 29th April 1935, when they lost 2-0 at Plymouth Argyle. The attendance of 3,000 produced match receipts of £65 for the Albion club.

A Polish Navy XI visited St James's Park for a friendly fixture with Exeter City Reserves on Saturday 1st November 1947. Their side included Poland International centre-forward Navrat who had been capped twenty five times for his country but the City Reserves won 4-0.

The game that finished five minutes too early! The referee, Mr E.G. Walliker of Salisbury mistakingly blew his whistle to signal the end of Exeter City's match with Gillingham in March 1953 five minutes too early. His error was pointed out to him by a linesman and some of the crowd at St James's Park. The match resumed, with Exeter holding on to their 2-1 advantage.

A party of seventeen Ugandan Chiefs undertaking a study tour of the South West attended City's game at St James's Park with Watford in September 1956. The public address system completely failed prior to kick-off with no team changes being announced, or music being played. Following heavy rainstorms, water had seeped into the control hut and short circuited the entire system.

Three members of the Icelandic Parliament were guests of the club for Exeter City's match with Bristol City in March 1965. Accompanied by Devon County Council officials, they were on a three week visit to England.

The half-time interval was extended to thirty minutes by match referee Mr E. Wallace. This followed a rainstorm, thunder and lightening, which had waterlogged the Somerton Park pitch during the course of the first half between Newport County and Exeter City in February 1969. The referee made two pitch inspections during the 'long' half time. The rain stopped, but the pitch was just a sea of mud. Mr Wallace astounded everyone, including both sets of players, by allowing the game to continue. Newport were leading 2-0 at the interval, with John Kirkham pulling back a goal for City in an energy sapping second half as the players ploughed their way through ankle deep mud.

History sometimes has a habit of repeating itself. This is certainly the case as far as Grimsby Town versus Exeter City matches are concerned. Twice the City have travelled to Grimsby for their final match of the season, and on both occasions played before 'large' attendances as Grimsby Town celebrated promotion.

The first occasion was in May 1972 when 22,484 spectators packed into Blundell Park to cheer Grimsby on to the Fourth Division championship. The home team needed just one point to clinch the title, and they more than made certain of the honour as they defeated Exeter 3-0.

Nineteen years later – May 1991 – amidst equally as jubilant scenes, Grimsby Town won the Third Division Championship before a crowd of 14,225 after narrowly defeating Exeter 1-0.

When neighbouring Great Mills League side Exmouth Town reached the semi-final of the FA Vase in 1985, Exeter City were so concerned about the effect it would have on the attendance for their match on the same afternoon against Colchester United that they considered switching their Fourth Division game to a Friday night. Exeter also offered Exmouth the chance to stage the semi-final at St James's Park, but it was felt that the match should go ahead as planned at Exmouth's Southern Road ground to reward their own supporters in what was the biggest day in the club's history. City's match with Colchester went ahead on the Saturday afternoon, crashing to a 5-1 defeat before an attendance of 1,825 at the Park, whilst Exmouth Town triumphed 3-2 over Fleetwood Town in the semi-final first leg tie in front of 2,012 spectators.

Exeter City claimed compensation from Stockport County following the postponement of their match with them in August 1985. The Edgeley Park ground was closed for safety reasons, and the two clubs could not agree on an alternative arrangement. City's claim for compensation revolved around the fact that they had two players on a month's loan, twins Alan and Gary Kimble from Charlton Athletic. Because of the postponement they could not play, giving City one game less to assess their respective abilities.

Stockport County had offered City to switch the fixture to St James's Park, but this was turned down for Exeter felt that this would affect the attendances as three home matches would then have been played in a space of ten days. City were particularly annoyed that the first they had heard of the possible postponement of the game at Stockport was through a newspaper report.

The whole episode was related at a meeting of the Football League

Management Committee, who decided to take no action. They accepted the Stockport County's club explanation that they had no alternative but to postpone the match because the local police had deemed their ground unsafe to use.

The Exeter City team were late arriving for their fixture at Orient in March 1986. Heavy traffic in London had delayed their arrival at the ground, and the team sheet was handed to the match referee fourteen minutes later than the rules allow. The matter was dealt with by the Football League Management Committee.

Similarly the Exeter team were late in arriving for their match at Burnley in September 1989, heavy traffic again being the cause. City were therefore fined £50 by the Football League for handing their team sheet to the referee ten minutes later than the stipulated time before kick-off.

MEMBERSHIP SCHEME

A membership card was required to stand in the Cowshed area of St James's Park as from the 1988/89 season. This followed safety reports into football grounds whereby certain areas had to be designated for members only. Membership cards cost £1, and were valid for the complete season.

In November 1988 the Government announced that they were planning to introduce a nationwide compulsory membership scheme for all football League grounds. Exeter City had at that time around 1,900 membership card holders. The scheme would mean that special turnstiles had to be installed at St James's Park at a cost estimated to be around £60,000. Only valid cards would automatically operate the turnstiles to enable spectators to gain access to the ground.

The scheme would cost several thousands of pounds to implement, money that the clubs, particularly in the Third and Fourth Divisions, did not have. Membership cards were not welcomed in general by football supporters nationwide, and a great deal of lobbying against the proposed measures took place over the next few months. Following a wave of criticism against the scheme and its impracticality the Government finally abandoned the idea in January 1990. Exeter City continued however to designate the Cowshed a membership card holders area only and still operated the scheme in season 1991/2 when entry could only be gained to the Cowshed through turnstiles at the St James's Road end of the ground.

MUSICIANS

Harry 'Jazzo' Kirk who played for Exeter City between 1921 and 1927, was well known for his musical interludes. He could often be found playing the piano at functions which the team attended from time to time, or even after games. Kirk was also renowned for his monologues which kept his team-mates entertained. The inside forward had been signed from Plymouth Argyle, leaving St James's Park for a spell at Charlton Athletic.

Pre-match entertainment in the 1920s and 1930s often consisted of a band playing on the pitch. Regular performers were the Exeter City Military Band under the conductorship of Mr George Newman. However, for the first time at St James's Park for the game with Reading on 13th October 1934, the services of Mr Newman's band was dispensed with for the day, and "microphones were connected to the loudspeaker system so that music from the B.B.C. could be relayed to spectators."

George Newman's band in fact often travelled to away games and performed their repertoire on other grounds. In October 1919 for instance they teamed up with the Bristol band to entertain the crowd prior to the Bristol Rovers versus Exeter City fixture at Eastville. It was reported that the combined band of forty performers played a selection of music for an hour prior to kick-off.

Prior to the game at St James's Park against Portsmouth in March 1920, George Newman was joined by a Miss Florence Newman who sang soprano solos accompanied by the band on the pitch to entertain the crowd.

Jack Hylton, the famous dance band leader of the 1940s, became a shareholder in Exeter City Football Club in May 1945 following an appeal from his cousin, and former City player, Percy Hilton. Jack sent the club a cheque for £50 together with a share application form.

Well known trumpeter Eddie Calvert purchased £100 worth of Exeter City shares in April 1955. He was the cousin of City player Frank Houghton.

NAMES

What's in a name? Until the annual shareholders' meeting on Friday 3rd November 1972, the Football Club was known as 'The Exeter City Football and Athletic Company Limited'. But as from that meeting the name became, 'Exeter City Association Football Club Limited'. The change of official title followed a request from the Board of Directors.

NICKNAME

One of the most often asked question about Exeter City is, 'Why are they called the Grecians?' No one really knows, although several theories have been given. Exeter certainly possess the oddest nickname in the Football League which perhaps will never be explained with any certainty.

One suggestion is that the word 'Grecians' is a corruption of the British name in the Roman language for Exeter – 'Caerwysc'. The citizens of Exeter would therefore have been called 'Caer Iscuns', which was gradually altered over the years to become 'Grecians'.

Another explanation is that there stood in Sidwell Street at the formation of Exeter City in 1904, a silversmith's jeweller's shop called Sidney Herbert. Outside the shop was a clock and written on it was the word 'Grecians'.

Yet another possibility was the story about a group of urchins who frequented the old St James's Market. They were referred to as the 'Greasy Un's'. Over the years this became 'The Grecians'

OPPONENTS ♣ LAST

Barrow Football Club lost their place in the Football League at the end of the 1971/72 season, when they failed to gain re-election to the Fourth Division (Hereford United were elected in their place). Barrow's last game in the League took place at St James's Park in April 1972, and it ended disastrously for them, as they crashed to a 7-1 defeat. Exeter's goalscorers were Fred Binney who netted twice, Alan Banks, Graham Parker, Tony Morrin, John Neale, and an own goal from Bobby Knox.

In the 1991/92 season Barrow were playing in the G.M. Vauxhall Conference.

Official Programme 5p

EXETER CITY FOOTBALL CLUB

City

v BARROW

ST. JAMES' PARK, EXETER

Fourth Division

Saturday
29th April, 1972
Kick-off 3.00 p.m.

OWN GOALS

Crystal Palace full-back, Collyer, had the misfortune to score two own-goals in front of his home crowd, both in the first half, as Exeter City went on to win 4-3 on 14th September 1910. The goals had been the first conceded by Palace that season.

PENALTIES

Wing half Stan Cutting achieved the rare feat of scoring a hat-trick of penalties in a match for the Exeter City Reserves team against Worcester City. The Southern League fixture took place at St James's Park on 8th January 1949, with City winning 4-3. Cutting scored his goals in the 30th, 35th, and 65th minutes. The third penalty saw Cutting's initial shot being partially saved by the Worcester goalkeeper, but he followed up by netting the rebound to complete his hat-trick. Winger Dennis Hutchings scored the other Exeter goal two minutes from time.

Barry Pulman scored a hat-trick of penalties during the course of successive games. In September 1958 he netted once from the spot in the Exeter City Reserves' 3-2 win over Trowbridge Town, and then two days later scored twice with penalties in the 'A' team 2-1 victory against Newquay. Both matches were played at St James's Park.

One of the oddest penalties awarded against the City must surely have been at Reading in October 1971. City goalkeeper Bob Wilson gathered the ball, and then pushed it into the face of Reading forward Terry Bell who had stood in front of him. The referee immediately signalled a penalty, which George Cumming slotted home via the foot of the post to help give Reading a 3-1 win.

PLAYERS

On at least two occasions Exeter City have had to borrow a player from the opposition to make up the numbers. The first occasion occurred on the City Reserves' trip to the Torquay Town club in February 1911. The Reserves arrived one man short, so borrowed a player by the name of Chaffe from the Torquay club. Chaffe had the audacity to score for Exeter against his team-mates who, nevertheless, won 2-1.

The second occasion that City borrowed a player was for a pre-season friendly at St James's Park against Swansea Town in August 1967. Injuries and illness reduced the number of players that City could call on. They borrowed 18-year-old winger, Brian Grey, to play against his own team Swansea Town. Exeter found themselves 4-0 down at half-time, going on to lose the game 5-2.

Inside left Martin Golightly, who joined Exeter from Gateshead in 1912, was originally a fireman with the North Eastern Railway Company before being spotted by the Gateshead club playing in junior football.

Financial worries were believed to be the cause behind the suicide of former Exeter City player and inside forward Stanley Cowie, who was found drowned in the River Tyne in 1927. Gowie played for Exeter between 1914 and 1920, having been signed from Blackpool.

Glaswegian Jimmy Gray who played for Exeter between 1930 and 1936

For many years the entire Exeter City staff, directors and players, enjoyed a pre-season outing. Here in the mid 1930s two charabancs are seen ready to depart from St James's Park probably for a drive across Dartmoor, always a favourite destination. The players are in the first vehicle, whilst the directors follow on behind.

moved to live in South Africa long before he came to St James's Park. After starring for Transvaal in an Inter-State match, he was persuaded to return to England by Liverpool. It was from there that he eventually signed for Exeter City.

Inside forward Ronald Boundy spent the 1933/34 season with Exeter City, making two league appearances. He scored in his final match for the City Reserves in a 2-1 Southern League win against Barry Town in May 1934. Ron was then released and signed for Southport. Sadly he never played again, for Boundy died after complications set in following a bout of pneumonia contracted after bathing near his Wallasey, Cheshire, home.

Another resident of Wallasey, after retiring from playing, was former Exeter City half back of the late 1920s Harry Gee. When City played at Liverpool in the third round of the FA Cup in 1950, the team stayed at a hotel in New Brighton, and Gee paid his old club a visit at their headquarters. He was then a newsagent and tobacconist in Wallasey and a local Borough Councillor. Another player to visit them was Jimmy Gray who made 213 appearances for Exeter between 1930 and 1936. Gray was working in a Liverpool Telephone exchange after the Second World War.

Exeter City half back Edward Keefe was awarded the Royal Humane Society's certificate in recognition of his brave action of saving Miss Ivy Rosaline Clark from drowning in the Exeter Canal in October 1934.

Full back Bob Wallace died on Monday 12th September 1938 following an operation to remove an abscess on his forehead. Wallace had two weeks earlier played in the opening League match of the season against Cardiff City. Signed from Plymouth Argyle in 1937, Wallace had made thirty eight league appearances for Exeter. A collection was taken at the next home match against Swindon Town to augment a fund which had been opened to help the player's widow.

The Exeter City players had to forego their usual bath after training in 1947 because of the Government's emergency fuel cuts. The boilers at St James's Park were then coal fired.

Many Exeter City supporters were bitterly disappointed at the non-appearance of Notts County's England centre forward Tommy Lawton for the Third Division South fixture at St James's Park on Saturday 14th February 1948. The attendance of 16,942 produced the then record club receipts of £1,312. Lawton had reportedly pulled out of the County team with gastric influenza, but his side still won the game 1-0.

The following season Lawton played in the Notts County team, but Exeter must have wished he had not! They crashed 9-0 on their visit to Meadow Lane on 16th October 1948, with Lawton netting four goals. In the return game at the Park the following March, Exeter gained revenge despite the presence of Lawton with a 3-1 win in front of 14,000 spectators.

Exeter City have had a few overseas-born players on their books and include Arthur Cooke and Glen Sprod (Australia), Joe Cooke (Dominica), Nelson Stiffle (India), Harry Boye-Karlsen (Norway), Basil Cook (South Africa), Antonio Cruz (Spain), Joe Auguste (Trinidad), John Baugh (Uganda), Hung Dang (Vietnam) and Folorunso Okenla (Nigeria).

Joe Cooke

The City Reserves team also played a gentleman by the name of Van Gelder in the 1946/47 season; although of an obvious Dutch origin, he was actually born in Paisley, Scotland!

It now seems almost unbelievable that players regularly took jobs during the close season. In the summer of 1948 for instance Exeter City players were busily engaged in a variety of occupations. Arthur Coles, Fred Davey and Bert Hoyle were working on local farms, whilst Ray Wright had an interest in a smallholding at Longdown. Harry Bartholomew, Cyril Johnstone and Doug Regan were employed in the building industry, and Angus Mackay was with a window cleaning company. Goalkeeper Barney Singleton was in the furniture trade, Stan Rowe in an engineering works and Bob Jeffrey was employed in the food industry.

In the close season 1962 eleven of the City players took jobs as lumberjacks with a forestry company at Chagford! They were Peter Gordon, Keith Harvey, Mike Hughes, Geoff Hudson, Alan Jones, Brian Jenkins, Les MacDonald, Arnold Mitchell, Derrick Sullivan, Eric Welsh and Brian Whitnall.

Between 1952 and 1966 Arnold Mitchell set a Football League appearance record for an Exeter City player by playing in 495 games. However at the end of the 1952/53 season Arnold was actually placed on the open to transfer list, but before any offers were forthcoming from any clubs City re-signed the player. He was to stay at St James's Park for another thirteen years!

The days of a big playing staff was over as far as Exeter City were concerned at the end of the 1959/60 season. They released or transfer listed an astonishing total of seventeen players, but still had another twelve who they retained! The 'fortunate twelve' were: Goalkeeper Alan Jones; Full backs Theo Foley and Les MacDonald; Half backs Arnold Mitchell, Keith Harvey, Jimmy Thompson and Peter Williams; Forwards Peter Bennett, Gordon Dale, Graham Rees, Eric Welsh and Jack Wilkinson.

No fewer than four players made their first team debuts for Exeter City in the Football League Cup-tie at Aldershot, a match which City lost 2-0. The debutants were full backs Bob Davis and Cecil Smyth, half back Bert Brown, and winger Hamilton McMeechan. Only Smyth made further appearances for the first team, going on to have 270 League outings.

Exeter City placed a transfer fee of £7,500 on forward Ray Carter in June 1963. Carter decided not to re-sign for City preferring to play for Southern League Crawley Town and take employment outside the game in a sports shop. The Exeter Board felt that the fee was not unreasonable in view of the fact that Carter had been the leading goalscorer in the two previous seasons. Although City continued to hold his Football League registration, Carter never returned to the higher level of the game.

Irishman Brian Symington turned down an offer from Dutch League champions, P.S.V. Eindhoven to join Exeter City in the l963 close season! The Irish Schoolboy International signed for City on a month's trial from Brighton and Hove Albion, earning himself a full contract at the end of that period. He never made the Exeter City first team and was released on a free transfer.

There was an English Rugby International on Exeter City's books during the 1963/64 and 1964/65 seasons. Wing half or inside forward Dave Hancock, who signed for City from Torquay United, played for the England Rugby Union Schools International side whilst at Hele's School. Hancock preferred to take up soccer and signed for Plymouth Argyle. He is one of the few players who have played for all three of Devon's Football League sides.

Ace City goalscorer Alan Banks arrived at St James's Park for Exeter's Football League Cup match with Gillingham in September 1964, to find he had no football boots! One of the ground staff had forgotten to collect them from the repairers. Exeter City programme editor, Maurice Golesworthy, came to the rescue! He collected the keys to the, by now, closed shop, retrieved Alan's boots and got back to the ground just four minutes before kick-off. The rush was worthwhile, for Banks scored the first of Exeter's two goals in a 2-0 win.

With Exeter City fighting against relegation to the Fourth Division in 1966

Some famous faces have played at the Park throughout the years. Seen here with Jimmy Giles and lad (centre) are Paul Mariner (left) and Charlie Nicholas.

– a battle they eventually lost – by the beginning of April of that year, no fewer than ten players were on the transfer list! They were Des Anderson, Pat Canavan, Dermot Curtis, Bryce Fulton, Les MacDonald, George McLean, Arnold Mitchell, Alan Riding, Cecil Smyth and Jeff Tolchard.

A most unusual tale unfolded in a magazine article which appeared in 1967 about former Exeter City winger John Cochrane. He had signed for the City in 1963 from Brighton and Hove Albion, having previously played for Irish League side Distillery. After playing a few matches for Exeter, including two in the first team, Cochrane realised that he had a problem with his eyesight. He admitted he could not always focus on what was going on around him in a game. He told City Manager Jack Edwards of his dilemma, and it was arranged for the player to wear contact lenses.

Alas! The lenses proved too troublesome and Cochrane dispensed with them. He had not wanted to tell the City manager any earlier of his poor eyesight for fear of being dropped from the team. City did eventually release the player and he returned to Ireland. The story has a happy ending, however, for on signing for Ards it was arranged for Cochrane to have smaller contact lenses fitted. It did the trick, and he won a regular place in the Ards team!

The Football League gave Exeter City special permission to play winger Brian Hart in their League Cup tie against Torquay United in August 1967.

They waived the rule whereby players had to be registered fourteen days before the game because the City had barely enough players fit enough to made up a team. Even with Hart being allowed to play, City had to make do without a substitute. Hart had joined Exeter on a trial period from Australian club, Corinthians. He was pitched straight into the City team after impressing in pre-season matches. Against all the odds, Exeter drew 0-0 at Torquay, but lost the replay back at St James's Park 3-0.

Car trouble plagued City's match with Chester in September 1968. Goalkeeper Peter Shearing's car broke down on the way to the ground at the village of Ide. Manager Frank Broome had to drive to Shearing's rescue and bring him back to St James's Park for the game.

That was not the end of it though. For John Newman failed to make the kick-off after being delayed in heavy holiday traffic on his way from Plymouth. He eventually made it to the ground twenty five minutes after the kick-off, by which time his place in the team was taken by Dermot Curtis, who was originally selected as substitute. Newman quickly changed and took over the substitute spot, and was then called into the action after fifty three minutes when Keith Harvey was injured. The result of the match? Honours even at 2-2.

Exeter City's goalscoring forward Fred Binney was twice stopped from entering opponents' grounds, officials refusing to believe he was a visiting player! The problem arose during the 1973/74 season when Fred took to

The City playing squad for the 1974/75 season. Back row (L to R) Peter Hatch, Michael Horne, Tony Ridley, Bob Wilson, Hedley Steele. Middle row (L to R) Jack Edwards (trainer), John Neale, John Templeman, John Rutter, Keith Bowker, Bobby Hodge, John Newman (manager). Front row (L to R) Graham Weeks, Nicky Jennings, Lammie Robertson, Keith Clapham, Brian Joy, Tony Morrin, Alan Hooker.

wearing a three-quarter length 'trench coat', which perhaps was just a little unfashionable for a footballer. The infamous coat had been bought by Fred whilst playing for Torquay United and was described as being better suited for a Siberian winter rather than the Westcountry climate.

He was first refused entry to the players' gate at Lincoln City, when the doorman was convinced that Fred could not have been a player. Luckily, the *Sunday Independent* sports writer, Gordon Hines, came to Binney's rescue and he was eventually allowed through. Binney then went on to prove that he was indeed a footballer by scoring a goal in the 2-2 draw.

Just seven days later a similar incident occurred at Cambridge United. This time an official would not allow Fred into the club's Vice President's Lounge with the rest of the Exeter City party. He couldn't be a player wearing a coat like that! Again Binney had the last laugh with another goal in Exeter's 3-1 win.

The professional playing staff at St James's Park defied an order given by manager John Newman in February 1974 which involved them doing extra training with the club's amateur players, including an evening session.

Newman had been upset at his players' attitude during a Western League fixture with St Luke's College. The virtual first team line-up were held to a 2-2 draw by the students. The players held a meeting at the ground and decided to refuse to comply with the manager's wishes.

Rhodesian right winger, 24-year-old, Bulawayo-born, Norman Ngwenya, arrived at St James's Park in March 1975 to train with Exeter City for five weeks. He played for South African First Division side, Moroka Swallows. He paid his own expenses to stay in England and asked to train with Exeter so that he could learn the English way of playing the game to take back with him to South Africa. He did however have an ambition: "I would play anywhere in this Country, and I would most like to play for Exeter City."

Two of the Exeter City team from the 1920s were the club's guests of honour for the game against Bolton Wanderers in October 1978. Goalkeeper Dick Pym and forward Harold Blackmore had been transferred from the City to Bolton in the 1920s, but both had returned to their native Devon surroundings at the end of their playing careers. The Bolton game was the first floodlit match that Pym had seen, whilst for Blackmore it had been the first match he had attended for twenty years.

Britain's first million pound footballer made his debut for his new club, Nottingham Forest, in February 1979 at Exeter City. Trevor Francis came into the fray as a second half substitute during the testimonial match for City winger Nicky Jennings between the Exeter and Forest. The appearance of Plymouth-born Francis, who had been signed by Nottingham Forest from Birmingham City, boosted the attendance to 9,479 which produced receipts of around £12,000.

Dutch Under-23 International Frans Koenan made his debut for Exeter in the unlikely homely surroundings of the Cullompton Rangers ground! Koenan had joined City on trial after being released by Newcastle United, who had earlier paid £80,000 for the player from Dutch club, Nijmegan. The game at Cullompton in November 1981 was to mark the official opening of their new social club, however City's opponents were not Cullompton, but Bridgwater Town. Koenan did not impress and was released by Exeter.

England winger Peter Taylor's short two month stay at Exeter City ended after a disagreement with the Board of Directors over financial arrangements. The final straw, however, was believed to have occurred when a director allegedly criticised Taylor's display in front of the players' family after an FA Cup match at Maidstone United. He left the club in December 1983 to return to the club he had been signed from, ironically, Maidstone United!.

Exeter City Winger Martin Ling captained the England Youth side against the England Public Schools XI in December 1983. Seven years later, Chris Vinnicombe, who had left Exeter for Glasgow Rangers in 1990, captained the England Under-21 international side.

Midfielder Symon Burgher turned his back on football in 1985 to follow his religious beliefs which prevented him from playing on Saturdays. Burgher, Birmingham-born, had progressed through City's youth scheme to make his debut against Aldershot in January 1985. He made a total of eleven Football League appearances, plus one as substitute.

Triallist Ian Wadsworth from Huddersfield Town netted seven goals in his first two matches for Exeter City Reserves in April 1986, including five in one game against Cardiff City. He made one substitute appearance for the City first team in a Devon Professional Bowl match a month later at Plymouth Argyle, but was not signed on for the following season.

PORK PIES

Whilst changing trains at Bristol Temple Meads station, one of the Exeter City players decided he would buy a couple of pork pies to eat on the rest of the journey to Burnley, where Exeter were due to play an FA Cup-tie in December 1910.

Nothing unusual in that you may say? But at Manchester railway station where the travelling party took another break in the journey, great confusion arose over those pork pies! The director in charge ordered drinks all round. The moment for cash settlement came, and the assistant charged for the drinks and two pork pies. "Two pork pies!" exclaimed the director, "I didn't order any pork pies." But the assistant promptly pointed to a player who was tucking into those pies he had bought at Bristol. The director was forced to settle the bill despite heated protests from the player. Those pies proved rather expensive for the player who, having paid for them at Bristol, then had to reimburse the director who had also paid for them in Manchester!

POSTPONEMENTS

In November 1906 the night before Exeter City were due to travel to Tavistock in a Plymouth and District League fixture, Sidney Thomas, the club secretary received a telegram to the effect that Tavistock had been suspended by the Devon County Football Association. The game was therefore postponed.

The Watford team were unable to travel to Exeter for a Southern League fixture in September 1919 due to a railway strike. There was no option but to postpone the game. In place of the Watford game, City hastily arranged a friendly fixture at St James's Park against local side Friernhay, winning 7-1. Friernhay themselves were due to play the Church Institute at Exmouth, but found that there were no vehicles available to transport the team, so were quick to take up the offer of a match against the City.

On the same afternoon, because of the rail strike, the Exeter City Reserves team were unable to fulfil their Plymouth and District League fixture in Plymouth against the Royal Naval Barracks.

Exeter City have twice had to cancel games against clubs that have gone out of business! On 2nd December 1950 City Reserves were due to play Chingford in a Southern League fixture at St James's Park. That game was called off however on the previous Wednesday when Exeter received a simple note from the Chingford club stating: "Very sorry we shall not be able to visit you on Saturday. You had better have a word with Mr Dickenson. Apologies for this curt note".

Mr Dickenson, the Southern League secretary explained to the City that Chingford Football Club had folded because of their mounting financial problems. The message from Chingford was not even written on headed club notepaper, but on the letter that Exeter City secretary George Gilbert had originally sent to them for details of their likely team!

A similar thing happened upon the demise of Accrington Stanley Football Club in l962. Exeter City were due to travel to Peel Park to play the Stanley on Saturday 10th March 1962, but the Accrington club were forced into liquidation four days earlier. Perhaps somewhat mercilessly, the City, rather than expressing their sorrow at the demise of Accrington, seemed more preoccupied on how much money they would save by not having to travel to Lancashire! They stated that if the game had gone ahead, travelling and hotel expenses would have come to £160, whilst the guarantee from match receipts would have been only £100, therefore a loss of £60 would have been incurred.

PROGRAMMES

The style of programmes have changed remarkably since the first ever issue at St James's Park. This was believed to be on sale for an Exeter City match in 1908. It then consisted of a piece of pink coloured paper folded in four, concertina style when opened. This type of programme was the standard issue until the Second World War.

On resumption of football in 1945/46, the more traditional looking football programme was produced, being the equivalent of today's A5 size. It was still small in terms of pages in comparison to what we now expect.

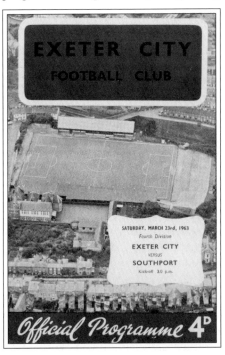

SATURDAY, MARCH 23rd, 1963
Fourth Division
EXETER CITY
VERSUS
SOUTHPORT
Kick-off 3.0 p.m.

Official Programme 4ᴰ

Various designs were used for the front cover. A player in red and white hoops, a view of Exeter Cathedral, a birds eye photograph of the ground – all have been used at one stage or another.

In recent years, programmes have become more like magazines, and of course have risen greatly in cost to buy. At the start of the 1956/57 season for instance, the cover price was increased from 3d to 4d. Inflation raised that price to 80 new pence (or a matter of 16 shillings in the old currency!), by 1990/91. It has to be said however that the 1990/91 issue was the best to come out of St James's Park for some time and a credit to all who were involved in its production.

For many years into the 1960s the Exeter City programme was edited by local statistician and author Maurice Golesworthy. It was always an informative read, which is more than can be said about the issues during the the 1980s which were not especially inspiring, with little content, and being very much advert laden. Indeed the issue for the 1984/85 season was described in a national magazine as being: "Desperate in design, very limited content, and minimal colour."

One of the biggest and most complete collections of Exeter City programmes belongs to Hugh Elwood, who needless to say is also something of an expert on the subject! His collection of home and away issues, pre and post war, includes many obscure friendly fixtures played by both the first and reserve teams. He has virtually a complete set of all games (not just League and Cup), played by Exeter City since the War. Amazingly, Hugh has not lived in Exeter since the early 1960s, and now resides in Gosforth, Newcastle Upon Tyne.

The collecting bug started after he attended his first Exeter City match during the 1958/59 season, and it has grown and grown ever since. He left Exeter to train as a teacher, and spent sixteen years living in Liverpool, before moving to the North East. Hugh does however make a regular pilgrimage to watch the City on their away travels anywhere in the North of England. His collection is very valuable, with prewar Exeter programmes worth anything up to £50 each and more, and even programmes from the early 1950s fetch £5 each.

PROMOTION — THE FIRST TIME!

The first major honour that Exeter City won in their history (apart from winning the Third Division South Cup in 1934), was promotion to the Third Division in 1963/64. That notable achievement will be forever fondly remembered by all those present at the historic match that ensured promotion. City could hardly have made a longer journey to fulfil their final fixture – one that took them to Workington. Despite the distance involved there were a good gathering of Exeter supporters who were determined to be present at the possible historic occasion on Saturday 25th April 1964.

British Railways offered a special excursion fare for the 800 mile round trip of 70/- (£3.50), from Exeter to Workington. The journey involved leaving Exeter St David's at 5.30 p.m. on the Friday evening. Another forty members of the Grecians Association preferred to travel overnight by coach leaving Exeter at 11.30 p.m.

The team also left on the Friday and when they arrived at their Carlisle hotel several good luck messages were waiting for them. These included one from former full back Bob Pollard, another from the Exeter Bowling Club, and even one from a long distance City fan in the Canary Islands! The following afternoon when the players walked into their dressing room at Workington they found another pile of good luck telegrams and cards, including one from Exeter Rugby Club.

Workington, were themselves already assured of promotion, and a good crowd of 8,600 packed into the small Borough Park ground. The result was a goalless draw, and the Exeter City promotion celebrations then began in earnest! With both sides having clinched promotion the Workington pitch was engulfed by jubilant supporters of both sides, chanting the players names.

Each of the Workington and Exeter City players appeared in the directors' box one by one to the enthusiastic cheering of the crowd.

The champagne and whisky flowed in the Exeter City dressing room. Later when the team returned to their Carlisle hotel they found that the hotel management had added to the occasion with a special cake being presented to the players in City's colours, with 'Well Done City!' iced on the top.

Many of the City supporters travelled back to Exeter on the same train us the triumphant team. They made their presence known when changing trains at Crewe station at 12.30 a.m. by cheering loudly, and did so again as they arrived at Exeter on Sunday morning, weary but ecstatic.

The welcome at St David's that the team received has not been repeated. It took the players fully half an hour before they managed to make their way through the throngs of people acclaiming their team's success.

Exeter City were given a civic reception the following evening at the Guildhall, where the Mayor of Exeter, Alderman W.G. Daw said: "As a former player myself and a keen supporter, I am delighted that you have got promotion in my year of office. I congratulate all the players and I am sure Exeter is very proud of you all indeed."

The team for that historic match at Workington had lined up as follows: Alan Barnett, Cecil Smyth, Les MacDonald, Arnold Mitchell, Keith Harvey, Des Anderson, Graham Rees, Alan Banks, Dermot Curtis, Dave Hancock, Adrian Thorne.

An occasion and a team that will forever be recalled by all those who were fortunate to be present!

Promotion – the Second Time!

Along with Workington (who finished in third position) and Exeter City (4th), both Gillingham (champions), and Carlisle United (runners-up), were also promoted to the Third Division. Sadly, Workington's success soon turned into despair. They were relegated back to the Fourth Division in 1967, and even worse was to follow. Ten years later Workington lost their Football League place after languishing in the bottom four of the Fourth Division for four consecutive seasons. They failed to gain re-election and were replaced by Wimbledon. In the 1991/92 season Workington were playing their football, still at the same Borough Park ground, but in Division One of the H.F.S. Loans League (formerly known as the Northern Premier League).

PROPERTY

Exeter City owned a number of club houses for players up until the late 1960s. One of the properties they owned was the house adjacent to the current entrance in Old Tiverton Road. This was purchased in the summer of 1948 with two ideas in mind. Firstly, it would be easier to persuade players to move to Exeter City if they could be offered accommodation to rent. Secondly, the purchase of the house and the adjoining land would overcome the difficulty that the club had in constructing a new entrance to the Big Bank end of the ground – i.e. the present Old Tiverton Road entrance.

The asset value of Exeter City's club houses in November 1950 was stated to be £9,800.

In November 1963 Exeter City chairman Reg Rose declared the club's intentions to replace the older players' club houses. He once again stressed the importance of the City owning such properties which made it easier to attract new players to the club. Three new houses had been purchased during the year.

PROSPECTUS

When Exeter City issued shares and turned professional in 1908, the prospectus for the new company showed that the company secretary was Mr Sidney Thomas, and the following gentlemen were to be directors of the club: Mr William Fenwick – An Accountant, Bloomtree Terrace, Exeter; Mr Frederick James Harvey – A Gentleman, West Avenue, Pennsylvania, Exeter; Mr Augustus Norman Kendall – A Gentleman, Queen Street, Exeter; Mr Michael McGahey – A Solicitor, St Johns Road, Heavitree, Exeter; Mr Thomas Oliver – A Licensed victualler, 117 Sidwell Street, Exeter; Mr Frederick Parkhouse – A Grocer, 109 Blackboy Road, Exeter.

The Exeter City Football and Athletic Club Limited was formed with a share capital of £3,000 divided into £1 shares. The company offices were shown as 21 Queen Street, Exeter. The articles of the company provided that if it should at any time have to be wound up, any surplus assets, after repaying the shareholders, should be given to another Devon or Exeter based club with similar sporting aims.

The Prospectus stated that as there were no professional teams nearer than Bristol or Plymouth, the club would draw its support from the towns of Crediton, Dawlish, Exmouth, Honiton, Newton Abbot, Sidmouth, Teignmouth, Tiverton, and Torquay. It went on to point out that prior to 1908 Exeter City had been a successful amateur club attracting between 3,000 and 5,000 spectators, but as a professional club gates would greatly increase.

It was proposed to lease St James's Park for twenty one years, at a rent of £100 per year, from the summer of 1909. Plans had been prepared to show the building of a Grandstand. A total of 18,000 spectators could be provided for in the ground. It was further proposed that in the summer months St James's Park could be used by the company for sports events, flower shows and band concerts.

Interestingly the company's objectives were also to promote a number of other sports – Athletics, Bowls, Cricket, Cycling, Golf, Hockey, Lacrosse, Motor Car Racing, Polo, Quoits and Tennis.

PUBLICANS

A number of Exeter City players have become Publicans after retiring from playing or leaving the club. They include Harry Bartholomew (Lamb Inn,

John Delve (middle) and Tony Kellow (left) became pub landlords. Pat Wakeham (back) and Dave Pullar (right) complete a happy quartet.

Exwick, Exeter), Cliff Bastin (Horse and Groom, Heavitree), Bill Brown (First and Last, Exmouth), Stan Cutting (Globe Inn, Exeter), John Delve (Village Inn, Exwick, Exeter), Micky Fudge (Lord Hill, Dawley, Telford), Ray Goddard (publican in Wolverhampton), Alf Green (Coach and Horses, Sidwell Street, Exeter), Bert Hoyle (Ship Inn, Cockwood, Starcross), Tony Kellow (Clifton Inn, Exeter), Angus Mackay (Locomotive Inn, Longbrook Street, Exeter), Jim McNichol (Exeter Inn, Ashburton), George Shelton (Bull Hotel, Goldsmith Street, Exeter), Steve Walker (Publican in Warminster), Ray Wright (Bath Arms Hotel, Frome, where he also managed the local club, Frome Town).

Defender Jim McNichol took over the Exeter Inn at Ashburton in May 1986, but Exeter City manager Colin Appleton felt that his football could possibly suffer as a result and only offered the player a three month contract a couple of weeks later. McNichol was not at all happy with the decision and promptly signed for Torquay United. He not only proved that the decision by the manager was a wrong one, but later returned to St James's Park in 1989, where he stayed for another two seasons. After the briefest of returns, yet again to Torquay, this ever-popular player retired from the full-time game in 1991.

PUBLICATIONS

Other than the usual sources of publications such as newspapers, match programmes, and club handbooks, there has been surprisingly little published detailing the fortunes of Exeter City Football Club.

Two newspapers were issued by the Exeter City club. The first, in 1977, celebrated promotion to the Third Division, whilst another was published to mark the club's 75th anniversary in 1979.

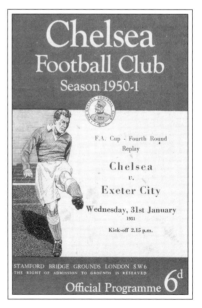

Perhaps the oddest publication that Exeter City have ever been featured in was a copy of *Japan News*! An edition of the newspaper was sent to the club by an exiled supporter serving in Japan with the forces in 1951. It carried a photograph of City keeper Barney Singleton saving from a Chelsea forward in the FA Cup fourth round replay at Stamford Bridge, which City lost 2-0.

Former Exeter City manager Jim Iley, slapped a ban on his players writing columns for the local Press in November 1984. He said: "As far as I am concerned the players who play for Exeter City are there to play football, and at this moment I want their energies channelled one way only towards the club."

Two players wrote columns at the time, full back Keith Viney for the *Express and Echo*, and striker Steve Neville for the *Exeter Weekly News*.

Most clubs now have Fanzines, which are not always approved of by the men in charge, but nevertheless they generally give the viewpoint of the supporter. Exeter City's Fanzine 'Exe Directory' first appeared in 1988 and has a large regular following of readers with regular issues being produced each season.

PUNCH AND JUDY

Exeter City took the unusual step of taking two teams who were to play each other in a pre-season match at Seaton in August 1922, and treated the occasion as a day out at the seaside. The entire party travelled from St James's Park on the Saturday morning, but stopped off on the way at Sidmouth. Some of the players took advantage of the break by watching cricket, whilst others were enthralled by a Punch and Judy show on the beach!

Lunch was taken at Trumps Cafe in the Winter Gardens, before the players moved onto Seaton where they were met by the chairman of the local Town Council. The game between the 'Red and Whites' and the 'Blue and Whites' produced five goals and a 3-2 win for the 'reds'.

QUOTES

There have been many 'prize' quotes made by persons connected with Exeter City Football Club. These have been made by directors, managers, and players, but perhaps the ones that are remembered for their originality and wit were those by Exeter manager Terry Cooper. Among the many gems that have appeared in the local Press are the following:

Commenting on Exeter City's performance after a 2-1 defeat at non-leaguers Bognor Regis in the FA Cup – "We were like a soggy Cornish pasty. At forty five years of age I could have gone on and done better and given more effort."

After imposing a club fine on striker Darren Rowbotham who had been booked for dissent in the game with Tranmere Rovers – "If we could play Darren in a muzzle we would be all right."

Following a 1-0 defeat at Rochdale and travelling City supporters chanting 'What a load of rubbish' – "If they are supposed to be our hard core supporters, then I hate to think what our enemies are like."

Commenting on the speculation surrounding a move for Chris Vinnicombe from Exeter to Glasgow Rangers – "That's the first I've heard of it. Somebody has got their wires crossed."

On completing the transfer of Chris Vinnicombe to Glasgow Rangers for a possible package deal of £400,000, just a couple of days after denying he knew anything about the move – "We've got Exeter City out of financial trouble and Rangers have got a future England International."

Explaining the story behind the signing of Tony Coyle on trial from Northwich Victoria – "I was cleaning the windows at home when it suddenly came to me, so I dashed up the motorway and did it."

About Scott Hiley after an outstanding performance for Exeter against Maidstone in February 1990 – "If I don't sell him for half a million I'll eat my hat. He's a different class to anything we have had here apart from Vinnicombe."

After a 3-0 defeat at York City – "Let's be frank. York absolutely stuffed us!"

Following the clinching of promotion to the Third Division in April 1990 – "I don't want to stay in football for the rest of my life, but I won't leave Exeter for any other club." He left to take over as Manager of Birmingham City in the summer of 1991!

RAILWAY TRAVEL

The Exeter City team have been involved in a number of incidents and mishaps whilst travelling to games by train. In March 1933 for instance, they were on their way to Reading for a Third Division South fixture when the train had to be diverted from its usual route to go via Swindon. With the kick-off time fast approaching, the players changed into their kit on the train, and when they got off at Reading West station were taken to Elm Park for the game by taxis. The rush did not appear to have too much effect on the team however, as City drew 2-2.

The Exeter City team were delayed after their match at Watford on 29th September 1951. Inside forward Richard Smart had been taken to hospital at the end of the game for stitches to a cut lip. Unfortunately by the time Smart had returned to join the rest of his colleagues, it left only forty five minutes to get from Watford to Paddington station to catch the 6.30 p.m. train back to Exeter. The City party got to Paddington just in time to see the train pull out! Instead of arriving in Exeter at 11 p.m., they had to wait for the overnight train, and finally arrived back at 4 a.m. Smart was not a popular fellow!

The City Reserves team missed their train in London on the way to Kettering for a Southern League fixture in August 1956. The 12.18 p.m. St Pancras to Manchester express, which did not normally stop at Kettering, was halted specially to allow the players to alight. The Exeter side therefore managed to arrive in Kettering fifty five minutes before the kick-off. They lost the game 2-1.

On Boxing Day 1956 the City Reserves team travelled as far as Gloucester station when they heard that their Southern League match at Worcester City had been called off. There were seven inches of snow lying on the Worcester pitch. The Stationmaster at Gloucester had obligingly held the Cornishman express train for a few minutes to save the Exeter players a long wait for a train back to Devon.

When Exeter City arrived at Walsall station in December 1958 a porter handed manager Frank Broome a message saying that the game with Walsall was called off. A telephone call from the station to Fellows Park confirmed this. The City party then travelled onto the Hawthorns for the West Bromwich Albion versus Luton Town match, but they were obviously out of luck that day, for even this game was abandoned in the seventieth minute because of the state of the pitch!

Exeter had a nightmare journey home from Stockport County in December 1962. The team left Manchester, after losing 4-3, by the midnight train. A couple of snowploughs and an extra steam locomotive helped the train arrive at Exeter St David's. It was the first morning train to reach Exeter after battling through blizzards and snowdrifts. The train was at least warm, and there was plenty of tea aboard, but the City players had not eaten since 6 p.m. on the Saturday, eventually reaching Exeter on Sunday afternoon! The train should have arrived at 9 a.m.

It was not the end of the nightmare journey for half back Keith Harvey. He managed to get a taxi as far as Newton St Cyres, and then had to walk through deep snow for the last four miles to his Crediton home.

In September 1963 Exeter City announced that in future they would not be travelling to away fixtures by rail. They must have had a change of heart for they were 'back on the trains' seven months later for their most important match in the club's history at Workington which clinched promotion to the Third Division.

The decision to stop going by train was taken by the Board of Directors on the grounds of cost. Instead they intended to go by road and have a coach fitted out with swivel seats and tables.

Exeter City secretary Keith Honey commenting on the club's decision said: "As far as we are concerned British Railways have priced themselves out of business. Most of our fellow Fourth Division teams are in the North, so we face a great deal of travelling. From bitter experience we have found we cannot trust the railway timetables. This means we can never afford to leave ourselves just thirty minutes for changing trains anywhere. We have to get there on time or face a heavy fine from the Football League for being late. There is no reduction in the dining cars for parties, but now we are going by coach we can book meals in advance in hotels on the way, at about half the price."

REFEREES
A tragic incident occurred during the Exeter City and Stockport County match at St James's Park in September 1972. In the sixtieth minute the

referee, Mr Jim Finn, of Chigwell Row, Essex, collapsed in the middle of the pitch. He had complained at half time of chest pains and was seen by a doctor. Mr Finn was carried off the field on a stretcher, and taken to to hospital, but was dead on arrival.

The game continued, not knowing of the seriousness of the incident, with linesman Mr Trevor Payne taking over as referee, and Exeter official Bill Dymond ran one of the lines. At the end of the match it was announced to the spectators that Mr Finn had died, and they were asked to leave the ground in silence as a mark of respect.

RESERVES

Despite denials following a national newspaper report in 1959 that sweeping changes were about to be made at Exeter City for the following season, the Board of Directors then issued a statement: "At a meeting of the Board on 3rd December, it was agreed by all the directors present that the club should withdraw from the Southern League and South Western League, and that an application should be made to enter the Western League. It was clearly shown in the last balance sheet that the club was facing tremendous difficulties with hotel and travelling expenses. The attendance at Southern League games have shown a serious decline over the past three seasons. The Board agreed that the above mentioned changes will help to meet today's additional expenses and by slightly reducing the personnel at the club at the end of the season, it will enable them to pay increased wages to the men retained. It is the intention of the Board to bring Third Division football to Exeter City as soon as possible."

Club chairman George Gillin added that City took an average of £40 from Reserve home gate receipts and that the Reserves cost approximately £200 per week to run.

An even more drastic step was taken at the end of the 1965/66 season, when chairman Les Kerslake announced that the club would only operate with one team the following season, and with a staff of between sixteen and seventeen players. The Western League and Exeter and District League teams would be disbanded. Mr Kerslake commented: "This is not a negative step, but positive action to concentrate all the efforts of the club into a successful Football League side. This policy has been adopted successfully by other League clubs, notably Portsmouth."

He went on: "This decision has been taken as a direct result of the lifting of the maximum wage restriction for players, and the introduction of selective employment tax."

Successful negotiations were held with St Luke's College so that the students could use St James's Park for their Western League fixtures. This would ensure that there was football at the ground on most Saturdays.

The Exeter City Board of Directors were confident that the economies made to run just one team would not only save several thousands of pounds, but also mean that some of the saving would be diverted towards team building. It was to prove a false economy, however, and the City struggled in the Fourth Division without a reserve team for the next six years before the policy was eventually reversed.

The lad on the bottom left of this photo is obviously a keen supporter as he is also featured in another picture on the front cover of this book!

Attendances for reserve fixtures in the 1930s, when Exeter City played in the Southern League, were far larger than those of today. Whereas City Reserve games now rarely attract more than one hundred, the matches in the 1930s were often watched by crowds of between 1,500 and 2,000.

ROYALTY

Two minutes silence was observed by the Exeter City and Newport County teams before the commencement of their Third Division South fixture at St James's Park on Saturday 25th January 1936. This was a mark of respect following the death of King George V who had died the previous Monday. Teams, officials, and supporters then sung the late King's favourite hymn, 'Abide With Me', followed by the National Anthem.

A similar mark of respect was paid in February 1952 by the Exeter City and Watford teams prior to their game at St James's Park after the death of King George VI, and again in March 1953 by the City and Southend United teams following the death of Queen Mary.

RUGBY LEAGUE

Exeter City's Fourth Division match at Barrow in March 1963 had the earlier kick-off time than usual of 1.45 p.m. to avoid clashing with the local derby Rugby League Cup fixture played between Barrow and Workington. After City had beaten Barrow 2-0, the entire party dashed across to the Rugby League ground by courtesy of the Barrow club who had sent across a batch of complimentary tickets.

ST JAMES'S PARK

St James's Park was sold to Exeter City Football Club for a bargain £40 in 1906 by Mr Albert Bradford who also owned a butcher's business in Sidwell Street. In 1991 St James's Park was estimated to be worth between £4–5 million! The plot of land was appropriately known as 'Bradford's Field' until 1906, and was not only used by local football teams but also rented out to various organisations for fund raising ventures. The Fire Brigade for instance held a well attended fete at Bradford's Field. Circuses also used the field.

The land was also used as a grazing area for sheep and cattle, the animals then being subsequently slaughtered and sold in the Bradford family butcher's shop. Unfortunately the shop was destroyed during the night of May 4th 1942 when an incendiary bomb dropped by a German warplane set the premises alight together with the adjoining buildings.

A reference to St James's Park was made by the *Express and Echo* newspaper in 1905, so the Exeter City club may well have adopted that name for the ground even before they had purchased 'Bradford's Field' twelve months later. It was further reported that the playing surface had been levelled and drained during the summer of 1905, with match reports of the time often referring to a slope before the work was carried out.

In August 1991, the son of Albert Bradford – Mr Bert Bradford, aged 67, made a nostalgic return to St James's Park. Living in Sussex it was Mr Bradford junior's first visit back to the ground for thirty four years.

Following a meeting held at the Red Lion hostelry in Sidwell Street in March 1908, the Exeter City Football Club Committee accepted terms for a twenty one year lease on St James's Park. At the same meeting it was also agreed to promote the scheme for the formation of a limited company.

It was discovered in season 1910/11 that the St James's Park pitch was in fact not long enough to stage FA Cup-ties. Exeter even had to give up ground advantage when drawn at home that season, being forced to travel to Nelson in Lancashire for a tie. Having successfully beaten them they were then drawn at home to Burnley. The City directors had the idea of re-marking the pitch at an angle, but when this was attempted it was still found to be three yards too short. The directors then approached the owner of the land behind the Big Bank end of the ground in an effort to extend the pitch. Exeter could not agree with him a price they could afford. City therefore had no choice but to switch the Cup game again to Burnley's ground. Burnley, incidentally, like Nelson, had refused a compromise of playing the game at the County Ground in St Thomas. Exeter were duly knocked out of the FA Cup, losing 2-0.

Negotiations were started for the possible move of Exeter City from St James's Park to the County Ground, but this was not pursued. The Football Club felt that it was unsportsmanlike to oust the long established Rugby Club from its headquarters.

The local Member of Parliament came to Exeter City's rescue in the Summer of 1911. Mr Duke very generously purchased the land that the club required, but could not afford, allowing the City to extend their pitch to the required length. In turn, Mr Duke was asked to nominate someone to represent him on the Board of Directors, this being a Mr F.G. Hill.

The newly lengthened pitch was used for the first time for a Southern League fixture with West Ham United. A crowd of 7,000 assembled to see a ceremony take place before the kick-off. Miss Duke cut a red and white ribbon which stretched across the space dividing the old and new portions of

Ground improvements being made to the Big Bank

ground. The crowd then saw a thrilling match which ended in a 3-3 draw.

A scheme to provide covered spectators' accommodation opposite the Grandstand was drawn up by the Supporters Club in 1919. It was described as being 'a form of shelter to accommodate about 5,000 people.'

On June 24th 1921 Exeter City, after their first season in the Football League, purchased the St James's Park ground consisting of 3.7 acres for £5,000. Most of the money was raised from the sale of goalkeeper Dick Pym to Bolton Wanderers.

During the summer of 1932, Exeter City completed the roofing of the area now known as the 'Cowshed'. Spectators paid the princely sum of one shilling to watch their favourites from their much improved surroundings. St James's Park was described as being one of the coziest and compact grounds in the Third Division.

The ground was in a sorry state in May 1945 after it had been used in the war effort. The Big Bank was overgrown with weeds, and wooden buildings, used by the military, had been constructed on the terracing on the covered side. Lorries had been parked and driven over the playing surface during the war years leaving ugly scars on the pitch. The playing surface had even been used as a parade ground for American troops.

The Exeter City groundsman Harry Greenaway had a mountain to climb to get the ground ready for the resumption of league matches the following August. With a month to go before the new season a major operation to re-terrace the Big Bank was underway, and it was anticipated that when complete 12,000 spectators would be able to stand there.

Plans to terrace the small bank behind the St James's Road goal were drawn up in November 1946, and a new entrance to the ground at that end was built four years later. An extension of the terracing at the St James's Road end was also constructed in 1950, estimated to enable 1,000 additional spectators to be accommodated. Also in 1950 a new entrance from Well Street was built, and the players' recreational hut was removed from the covered enclosure to provide more terracing. All the improvements was estimated to have increased the overall capacity of St James's Park to around 25,000. Experts measured the terracing at the ground allowing eighteen inches for each person in comparison with the Home Office allowance of sixteen and a half inches. On these calculations the Park had room for 23,000 excluding the Grandstand.

A new entrance from Old Tiverton Road onto the Big Bank was constructed in 1950 at a cost of £613, which was paid for by the Grecians Association. It was used for the first time for Exeter City's FA Cup third round replay against Grimsby Town on Wednesday 10th January 1951, which attracted an attendance of 18,177.

The most signings Exeter City made in one day was in July 1956, when no fewer than thirty additions to the staff were made. No, not players, but thirty sheep! They were 'signed' to aid the St James's Park groundstaff in preparing the pitch for the forthcoming season. They were only on loan, however, for after a week of grazing their job was done, with the grass nicely cropped.

In an effort to raise much needed finance to clear pressing debts, Exeter City offered to sell St James's Park to the Exeter City Council in February 1961. They offered the ground to the Council for £60,000 with the proviso that the club could continue to rent or lease it, in perpetuity, at a nominal rent. The Council turned the proposal down.

An Exeter City supporter was very critical of the facilities at the ground in September 1966. In a letter to the *Express and Echo* newspaper he wrote: "If the Exeter City directors want support, then they must consider the ordinary four shilling supporter."

He complained of ancient terracing, rotting sleepers, and unlit and unbolted filthy toilets. On one occasion he had to leave the ground just before the end of a game but found that the exit gates were locked. This led him to clambering through the rows of Grandstand seats to find a way out.

A miscellany of expressions as spectators view a game from the Grandstand before safety improvements were made.

A number of improvements and alterations were made to St James's Park during the late 1980s and early 1990s after stringent safety regulations were introduced for football grounds. Further details can be found under the

'Ground Safety' section.

Gale force winds demolished the fencing alongside the railway embankment and the Well Street entrance to St James's Park in January 1990. The fencing which had been erected in the 1940s, was replaced on a temporary basis by a barrier of scaffolding poles.

In 1990 the possibility of selling St James's Park, and moving to a brand new all-seater stadium on the outskirts of the city, was raised. After visiting similar ventures by other clubs, it is noticeable that one thing cannot be recreated – that is years and years of history and more importantly a sense of homeliness. Atmosphere cannot be built, it can only be developed over a number of years. It would in many respects be a sad day if Exeter City left St James's Park. However, it is doubtful whether sentiment would even be considered as we live in an age when finance and safety dominates the game of football.

SCUNTHORPE UNITED SAGA

Described by many as one of the biggest injustices in modern day football, Exeter City Football Club were fined £5,000 and ordered to pay Scunthorpe United more than £1,000 for the non-fulfilment of a fixture in April 1974. The Football League announced their punishment despite the fact that the club had medical certificates to prove that they were unable to raise a team owing to players being injured or ill.

City were scheduled to travel to Scunthorpe for a Fourth Division fixture on Tuesday 2nd April. But with nine players sidelined through injury and illness they found it impossible to raise a team and contacted the Football League to seek a postponement of the game. This was refused. Exeter City chairman Gerald Vallance and his fellow directors took the decision not to travel and they had the backing of the club doctor, Byron Pepper, who said: "In my view the club is perfectly correct in refusing to put these players at risk. I have issued nine certificates to be forwarded to the Football League confirming that these players are not fit to play. Last Saturday Exeter City were forced to field a team against Peterborough United in which at least two players should not have played because of illness. They suffered physical reaction afterwards."

Ironically, Halifax Town, only days before, had a game postponed with the blessing of the Football League when they too were hit by injury, having only ten players available. Nevertheless the League would still not agree to Exeter's request on this occasion.

The nine medical certificates were issued for Fred Binney, Keith Bowker, Keith Clapham, Jimmy Giles, Tony Morrin and Graham Parker, all suffering from illness. Brian Joy, Tony Scott and Ken Wallace were also sidelined on doctors orders because of injury. With defender Mike Balson suspended, this left Exeter City with just nine available players!

The Scunthorpe United club were not at all happy with the action taken by Exeter. A spokesman said unsympathetically: "I would hope that we will get the points out of this, and of course, the possible matter of compensation, but that is entirely up to the Football League."

Scunthorpe United manager Ron Bradley added: "I don't see why we should suffer for this. I feel that the League should award the game to us. I am simply not prepared to accept Exeter City's excuse."

It was not without careful consideration that Exeter City took this drastic action. Mr Vallance consulted his opposite number at Torquay United Football Club, Tony Boyce, who was the Division Three and Four representative on the Football League. Mr Boyce vowed he would give the Club all the support he could. City twice asked the League for a postponement without success, the League's vice-president Bob Lord (also Chairman of Burnley), and Sam Bolton of Leeds United, pointed out that City must fulfil the fixture.

Exeter delayed their scheduled departure to Scunthorpe for two hours, before Mr Vallance announced: "I think that it would have been ludicrous to go all the way to Scunthorpe with nine fit men. I am sure the referee would not have allowed the game to go on. The Football League may fine us heavily, but they will look pretty silly if they do."

Exeter City were supported by several other managers throughout the League when they heard of the club's plight, including Malcolm Allison, and Joe Mercer. The latter said: "I cannot see how the Football League can make out a case against Exeter City. I feel sorry for Exeter City but I think common sense will prevail."

The Football League considered the case at their next meeting, and on 25th April announced their verdict that Exeter City Football Club would be fined, and also forfeit the two points at stake. This decision was reached despite medical evidence that players were unfit to make the trip to Scunthorpe! Mr Vallance immediately offered to resign as chairman of Exeter City taking the blame for the decision not to travel, but this was unanimously turned down by his colleagues on the Board.

Supporters and sponsors were angered by the decision and immediately started a fund to pay the fine. Exeter City threatened to take legal action against the Football League, and the fact that medical advice appeared to be ignored also greatly annoyed the club doctor. He reacted angrily by saying: "The League clearly think that they are better judges of the players' fitness than I am."

Exeter City eventually paid the fine after losing an appeal against the Football League's decision. The directors raised the money along with the substantial amount collected by supporters and sponsors. The *Sunday Independent* newspaper opened an appeal fund among their readers, and this raised £1,341. The whole saga left a bitter taste. Exeter City had been unfairly treated.

Mr Vallance said: "Many lawyers advised us to take the Football League to the High Court over the affair, but taking all things into consideration we decided against it. When we appeared before the League Management Committee it was no form of appeal. In fact we were told almost as soon as we entered the room that we had no chance of the fine being reduced. It was really a waste of time meeting the Committee."

SECRETARIES

Whilst Sidney Thomas holds the record as the longest serving Exeter City Football Club secretary, Scotsman Jimmy Cook had the shortest spell. He joined the club on 25th October 1960 from Montrose Football Club where he had held a similar position for the previous five years. Just twenty days later however, Cook resigned, saying he felt unsettled and returned to Scotland. Cook had in fact told the City Board of Directors after only a week in the job that he wished to go home but would stay until a replacement was found.

Mrs Patricia Smith became Exeter City's first female club secretary upon her appointment to the post in October 1964. She was also at the time the only woman club secretary in the Football League. Mrs Smith had lived in Exeter for four years and worked as a company secretary but had never been involved with a football club before.

Club chairman Reg Rose said that the directors were very pleased with her appointment and that Mrs Smith was very experienced in all aspects of commercial work. She would be guided by the club's accountants. Three months later however, Mrs Smith was sacked from the job.

Exeter City appointed their youngest ever Secretary, 21-year-old Mike Cosway, in July 1968. He also became at that time the youngest club secretary in the Football League. Mr Cosway had been supporting the City for a number of years, and the Board of Directors felt that by appointing a younger man, he could learn the job and would be likely to stay with the club for a long time.

That 'long time' became just over a year! Mr Cosway left the City for a similar appointment with Halifax Town. The Board, however, continued their policy of appointing youthful secretaries, as they named 21-year-old Mr Ian Tarr as his replacement in September 1969.

Mr Tarr didn't last much longer than Mr Cosway. He was sacked in April 1971, after being asked to resign by the club's directors but refused to do so as he saw no reason to! The club stated that they felt they needed someone older in the office and a more experienced person. This seemed a strange decision, as Exeter City had taken an awfully long time to find out that they needed an experienced Secretary – three years in fact! Mr Tarr, who later worked for Bristol Rovers in their Development Association, was immediately replaced by 48-year-old Mr Russell Thomas.

Mr Cosway returned to Exeter City in December 1971, this time as Assistant Commercial Manager. He had resigned his post as Secretary of Halifax Town so that he could return to Devon. Cosway later had a long spell as secretary and commercial manager at Aldershot Football Club, before returning yet again to Exeter City as secretary.

SENDING-OFF

The first reported player to be sent off in a match involving Exeter City was a member of the 111th Battery team in October 1904. The East Devon League match was, by all accounts, a rough affair and after City players Horner and Davidson were both injured in dubious tackles by the same player, the referee ordered the miscreant off the field amid much applause from the crowd. City won 5-1, the game being a personal triumph for Exeter's 'crack' forward, the Reverend Reid who scored all five goals!

Two Exeter City players were sent off in the same Southern League Reserve team game at Bath City on Easter Monday, 26th March 1951. Six minutes from time, Alan Short was sent off, and he was soon followed by the dismissal of Richard Smart. City Reserves lost 5-1!

Goalkeeper Hugh Kelly was sent off during the game at Bristol City in December 1952. A penalty was awarded by the referee against Exeter City and Kelly was booked for protesting and throwing mud at the ball. He then saved the kick taken by Albert Eisentrager but continued to protest and was promptly sent off. Centre forward Jimmy Dailey took over between the posts but Exeter went down 4-1.

Defender Ken O'Doherty made an Exeter City first team debut that he would no doubt rather forget. Signed from Huddersfield Town on loan in August 1991, his first game for the City ended in 6-1 defeat at Shrewsbury Town. Sadly for O'Doherty he didn't complete the match, being sent off early in the second half after fouling an opposing player. He was joined in the dressing room for an early bath twenty minutes later when another City player, Tom Kelly, was also sent off.

SHOTS

Needless to say various comments, mainly of the sarcastic variety, have been expressed at the standard of shooting by Exeter City players. One Exmouth-based supporter has for example described City's shooting in the 1962/3 season as being so bad that ball boys had to be stationed on the top of Bobby's (now Debenhams) building!

The City players tested a machine in September 1972 which could register the speed of an individual's shooting ability. Forward John Wingate proved to have the hardest shot at St James's Park when he recorded a speed of nearly

Exeter City's 1981/82 playing squad. Back row (L to R) Steve Davey, Frank Prince, Phil Roberts, Mike Lester, Lee Roberts, Alan Lisle, Ian Main, Len Bond, Ray Pratt, John Sparrow, Joe Cooke, Peter Hatch. Middle row (L to R) Chris Davey (youth development officer), Martin Rogers, Phil Fisher, Dave Pullar, Brian Godfrey (manager), John Delve, Malcolm Musgrove (trainer), Tony Kellow, Tony Mitchell, Peter Rogers, Alan Beer (coach). Front row (L to R) Jon Claypole, Graeme Kirkup, Nick Marker, Steve Taylor, Frank Howarth.

60 m.p.h. Winger Barry Rowan came second at 57.4 m.p.h., and defender Mike Balson third with 54.8 m.p.h.

Some wayward shooting during pre-season training in August 1922 had a shattering effect. In just one week, shots from Bill Devlin and Alf Green flew out of the ground into St James's Road, where one broke a street lamp, and the other a plate glass window in the nearby houses. The *Express and Echo* report of the incidents added that if only the players concerned could – 'cultivate direction, then heaven help the visiting goalkeepers.'

SNOW

The snow fell heavily during the Cambridge United versus Exeter City Fourth Division fixture in January 1976. The small crowd numbering just over 2,000 shivered, as the players did their best to overcome the unpleasant conditions. At one stage the ball went out of play and City midfielder Lammie Robertson approached the match referee suggesting the game might be abandoned. Fortunately, for City, the referee disagreed, and Mike Jordan later scored the only goal of the game to give Exeter the points.

SOCIAL CLUB

Exeter City were prevented from building a social club in November 1964 on land near the Old Tiverton Road entrance to the ground. Retired Metropolitan Police Inspector Victor Meek of 20 Old Tiverton Road, Exeter, brought the initial work to halt, the foundations having been dug, when he produced a covenant which prohibited such development.

The covenant between himself, as owner of number 20 Old Tiverton Road, and Exeter City Football Club as owners of number 18 Old Tiverton Road, stated that a building of that kind should not be erected. The covenant made in 1883 forbade any kind of building on that property except a dwelling house at the front or offices of a dwelling house at the rear.

Planning permission for the social club had been given by the Exeter City Council, who were aware such a covenant existed but said it did not affect planning permission and was a matter to be resolved between the parties concerned. Exeter City chairman Reg Rose denied he knew of any restrictive covenant, but Mr Meek said he would take the matter to court if the building work did not stop.

A few days later Mr Rose said that the Exeter City Board of Directors would not contest the 1883 covenant and instead they were to move the site of the social club to the practice pitch behind the Big Bank where, according to club solicitors, there was no building restrictions. The re-siting would cost City several hundreds of pounds, for planning permission would again have to be obtained, and the work which had already been carried out abandoned.

The Minister of Housing and Local Government was asked to make a decision on the revised plans by the Exeter City Council because they now received a large number of objections, around 200, to the social club scheme from local residents in the Old Tiverton Road area.

A public enquiry was held on 20th July 1965, and some eight months later Exeter City heard of the Minister's decision. His letter read: "The Inspector considered that although it might be reasonable to permit the erection of a small building on the site for use as administrative offices by the committee of the Supporters Club, and for the preparation of light refreshments to be prepared to serve during the course of matches played on the adjoining ground, it would be wrong to permit a clubhouse for social and other activities indulged in by members of the club."

The letter went on to list his main objections to the proposed clubhouse. Any subsequent extension would involve the encroachment on car parking space, leading to undesirable parking in nearby residential streets. The existing and proposed access to Old Tiverton Road was in a dangerous position with inadequate sight along a busy highway. He also felt that the increased noise generated by persons going to and from the club would disturb the residents at a time when it was reasonable to expect the district to be quiet.

In December 1970 the Exeter City Board of Directors announced that they were again investigating the possibility of building a social club, costing in the region of £10,000, on land behind the Big Bank. A number of breweries had been approached, and two had made offers of financial assistance.

Originally two sites for a social club were considered, for as well as land behind the Big Bank, a possible site was under the main Grandstand, which meant re-locating a number of offices. This latter idea was turned down on the grounds of cost involved. Lack of access and objections from nearby residents in Old Tiverton Road once again ruled out the site behind the Big Bank.

Work on building the long-awaited social club eventually began in June 1972. The adopted scheme cost £8,500 with the directors contributing £2,000, the residue being borrowed locally. The building was to be 64 foot long and 24 foot wide, and situated at the top of the Big Bank.

The Social Club, named 'The Centre Spot', was officially opened following Exeter City's pre-season friendly with Halifax Town on 13th August 1973. A steward was appointed, this being Exeter-born Fred Wright who had made a few appearances for the City 'A' and 'B' team a few years previously.

In 1979, the Social Club was re-located to its present site, behind the Big Bank – not far from the very spot where the original plan to build it had been rejected in 1964!

SOUTHERN LEAGUE

Exeter City were willing to play two Southern League matches on the same day on 8th December 1956. They applied for permission to the Southern League Management Committee to play the first team against Newport-based side, Lovells Athletic at St James's Park, and the Reserves would play the other fixture on the same afternoon at Bath City. The City first team were without a game that day, as they had been knocked out of the FA Cup. The Lovells club had willingly agreed to face the Exeter first team, but the Southern League vetoed the plan, and only the Bath game went ahead. Whilst the reserves drew 3-3, the first team travelled to Stockport County for a friendly fixture which ended in a 4-2 defeat.

SPECTATORS MEETING

It is a highly unlikely scenario today! In January 1911 the Exeter City Board of Directors consulted the supporters whether they objected to the plan to increase ticket prices for the visit of Plymouth Argyle. The week prior to the Argyle fixture the directors called a meeting at St James's Park immediately following the City Reserves' friendly with the South Staffordshire Regiment (City won 6-2). Around 2,000 spectators stayed behind to hear and agree the prices proposed by the Board. Club Chairman Mr McGahey told the spectators that the final decision rested entirely with those present. Eventually a near unanimous vote decided in favour of advance tickets being sold at the normal admission prices, but those who gained admission to the game on the day without tickets would have to pay double prices. For the record, the match with Argyle a week later, drew an attendance of 9,000 to the Park, Plymouth winning 3-1.

SPONSORSHIP

The first ever Football League match to be sponsored at St James's Park was between Exeter City and Torquay United on Boxing Day 1973. The sponsors were local travel agents, Park Travel. It was nearly ten years later before the first ever Exeter City pre-season friendly fixture was sponsored at St James's Park. Again it was against Torquay United on 10th August 1983. The sponsors were Rotolok of Bampton and City lost the game 1-0.

LCD Advertising became the first company to display their names on Exeter City shirts. The sponsorship deal was agreed at the start of the 1984/85 season, and was to include the following season as well. The deal was worth a projected £20,000. LCD's managing director was former Exeter City goalkeeper Alan Trump who first played for the club in 1965. He stayed for two seasons, returning for a second spell with City in 1974/75. The overall deal also included advertising and match sponsorship.

Electrical and Mechanical Engineers, T.A.J. Hibberd became the shirt sponsors in 1989/90. Trevor Hibberd, the company's managing director, a life-long supporter of the City, has his business near to the ground, in Prospect Park.

SUNDAY BLUES!

The first Sunday Football League fixture that Exeter City played was in the Fourth Division at Bradford City on 20th January 1974. In front of the

Yorkshire club's best attendance of the season – 9,041 – Exeter lost 1-0.

A week later City travelled to Newport County for another league match. Striker Keith Bowker became the first Exeter player to net a League goal on the Sabbath, but City still lost 2-1.

They played one further Sunday game, this time at Reading on 10th February 1974. Graham Parker scored for Exeter, but once again it was not enough as they crashed to a 4-1 reverse.

League football has never been played on a Sunday at St James's Park.

SUPPORTERS

Mr McGahey, the chairman of Exeter City, sent a letter to the local Press, in August 1930, after being disturbed at the increase in the barracking of players. It read: "The barracker is a cad, who in a music hall would be dealt with promptly and effectively. The job of restraining him is more difficult when he is in the midst of a crowd, like that at St James's Park, stood in the open air. It is not impossible though, and it is imagined that if the trouble persists Exeter City will not hesitate to take action."

David Denley of Pinhoe, Exeter was voted as Exeter City's Supporter of the Year in 1973, but within a month he vowed never to raise another penny for the club. He had raised £1,800 for the club with various schemes and then applied to purchase some shares, but was turned down by the Board of Directors.

Mr Denley said: "That is the end of my fund raising for the club. I am extremely upset and disheartened. I only wanted a maximum of £50 worth of shares. They would have not have been for my own personal profit. It was just to have some small part in the club."

Exeter City director Wally Rice replied by saying "The club did not have enough shares available." (In fact they had 480.) "We needed to keep shares back because we want to enlarge the Board."

One of the most unusual requests for an FA Cup ticket, received by Exeter City, was surely that for their sixth round tie at Tottenham Hotspur in March 1981. A postal request was sent direct to manager Brian Godfrey explaining that due to circumstances beyond the applicant's control, he would not be able to collect the ticket in person. He went on to say that, unfortunately, he was at the time being detained at Her Majesty's pleasure in Exeter Prison, but would however be released the day before the game in London!

Miss Brooke Chapman became one of the youngest, if not the youngest, official Exeter City supporter, when at just forty six days old, she was enlisted in the club's membership scheme for the terraces under the Cowshed! She was born on January 4th 1989, and saw her first match – a 3-0 win over Burnley – six weeks later. Her parents, Clive and Sarah regularly made the journey to St James's Park from their Southampton home, and began to bring young Brooke along with them.

SUSPENSIONS

The Exeter City Board of Directors took the then unusual step of suspending two players and the club trainer in November 1911 for a breach of discipline. Following a meeting of the directors, club captain Bob Watson, and forward Fred Parnell, together with trainer Jack Banks, were told that they were not required to attend the FA Cup replay at Merthyr Tydfil – which again ended all square, this time 0-0. A few days later, Watson resigned his position as captain, being replaced by Walter Whittaker.

TAKEOVERS

Virtually every Football League club must have been the subject of a takeover bid at some stage in their history. Exeter City are no different, with several attempts having been made.

A group of locally based businessmen were keen to take over the club in January 1965. Mr Les Kerslake, himself a former City director, acted as their go-between, but the Board of Directors rejected any advances.

In November 1986 former Plymouth Argyle chairman and Ascot-based millionaire, Ron Blindell, was approached by Exeter City to join the Board of Directors as chairman and in doing so invest a substantial sum of money in the club, thus giving him a controlling interest.

Mr Blindell visited Exeter for meetings with the directors, but after talks it was announced that any possible deal was off. Blindell said that the Exeter City Board of Directors had a change of mind after he had put certain proposals. This included him purchasing St James's Park for £20,000 and then renting it back to the club.

Former Exeter City chairman Reg Rose confirmed, in July 1970, that he had been approached by persons, including ex-directors of the club, to mount a takeover bid. He had been talking to interested persons over a period of six months. No formal offer, however, was received by the Exeter Board of Directors and nothing further was heard.

A group of seven businessmen, all resident in the Exeter area, revealed their intentions to take over the club in December 1979. They estimated that it would cost around £200,000 to gain a controlling interest. Once again nothing more was heard about the scheme which was rejected by the Exeter City directors.

A long running and often bitter saga over the control of the club involved Bampton-based businessman Dan McCauley. He had been voted off the Board of Directors after offering to inject a substantial sum of money by means of a share issue. His fellow directors disagreed with him, and Mr McCauley was removed from the Board.

There then followed a series of attempts between January 1984 and

January 1986 by Mr McCauley to take a controlling interest in the club. On one occasion he delivered a £100,000 cheque to the ground, but this together with all other attempts to gain control was rejected by the Board of Directors.

THOMAS, SIDNEY

Described as the pioneer of Exeter City Football Club, Sidney Thomas, was connected with the club for over forty years in various capacities, but notably as player and secretary. He started his playing career as a 15-year-old with St Sidwell's United, who won the Exeter and District League Championship two years running. Thomas was then appointed player-secretary of the St Sidwell's Club, which became Exeter City in 1904.

It was mainly through his determination that just four years later Exeter City were a professional club, and had progressed rapidly through the Plymouth and District League to join the Southern League. He was appointed company secretary on the formation of a limited company in 1908 and held that position until 1939.

TITANIC

The Exeter City club flag was flown at half-mast at the home match with Crystal Palace on 20th April 1912, in memory of all those who had perished with the sinking of the *Titanic*. A collection was made at half-time for the Titanic Fund, which was reported as being the largest ever sum raised at St James's Park totalling £10 12s 9d.

One of the passengers aboard the ill-fated *Titanic*, was former Exeter City player Harry Dyer, who played for the reserves prior to the club turning professional in 1908.

TOUR – HOLLAND

Exeter City have twice travelled to Holland for friendly fixtures. The first occasion in 1925 saw the City go down 5-1 to a strong Ajax side in Amsterdam. Twenty six years later however, in 1951, City faced a much more exhausting programme of matches. The team and officials were based at the Hotel Restaurant De Haas in Amsterdam for their four match tour of Holland. The son of the City secretary George Gilbert lived in Amsterdam and acted as liaison officer between the Ajax club, who were to be the hosts throughout the stay, and Exeter City and was responsible for most of the arrangements. On arrival in Amsterdam the City team were met and welcomed by the president of Ajax, whilst the Amsterdam Post Office Band played the National Anthem.

Exeter defeated D.O.S. Utrecht (3-0), Haarlem Eftal (5-3, a game in which winger Charlie McClelland netted a hat-trick), and a Combined Hague XI (2-0). They were however defeated by B.V.V. Hertogenbosch (4-2), where the start of the second half was delayed. The teams returned on to the pitch only to find the band still playing, determined to finish their piece of music. Then

The Exeter City party relax in an Amsterdam cafe before their friendly match with Ajax in March 1925. City defeated Ajax 5-1 in front of a crowd of 15,000. (Ajax did not win any major honours in the 1920s.)

the conductor asked, with the referee's agreement, to play an encore. The half-time interval was extended to twenty minutes

As well as playing football the City party toured a diamond factory and also the bulb fields. Before Exeter left Holland they were presented with mementos, by Ajax Football Club, which included clogs containing miniature bottles of spirits.

TOUR – SOUTH AMERICA

Much has been recorded of Exeter City's tour of South America in 1914 but there were several incidents of note that took place which are well worth recalling. They played eight matches with the following results: Argentine North (0-1), Rosarian League (3-1), Fluminese (5-1), Argentine South (3-0), Combinadoes (5-0), Brazil (3-3), Racing Club Buenos Aires (2-0), and Rio de Janeiro (3-0).

When Exeter scored against the Argentine Champions, Racing Club, the local secretary brandished a revolver and threatened to shoot the referee! The match official stopped the game, and it was only after a good deal of persuasion that he decided to continue.

City were leading 3-0 with ten minutes of the match remaining against the Rosarian League when the home side were awarded a penalty from which they scored. The crowd went wild with delight letting off fireworks, screaming and shouting. This was followed by the band marching onto the pitch to play the Argentinean National Anthem half a dozen times!

Exeter City goalkeeper Dick Pym broke a couple of ribs in the first game and his understudy Reg Loram played in goal for the rest of the tour. Pym did not enjoy the best of sea journeys from England to South America – he suffered badly from sea sickness on the outward crossing. This, despite the fact that he spent hours fishing out on the River Exe from his Topsham home, and was something of an accomplished sailor.

Some of the Exeter City team aboard ship on the way to South America in 1914. The view was taken by the official photographer of the Royal Mail Steam Packet Company.

Several of the Exeter City players were arrested for 'Indecent Exposure' on the beach at Rio de Janeiro. They decided to sunbathe and removed their shirts, as well as taking a dip in the sea in their football shorts. But this was regarded as being indecent and they were quickly arrested by the local police and taken away by tram for questioning! After much explaining through an interpreter the players were allowed to go without any charges being brought against them.

The tour, despite being a success results wise, was not so good according to one of the Exeter City directors, who on the last day in South America was reported as saying: "I shall be glad when we have gone. I've had a wretched time and so have the players. We are sick and tired."

Seventy years later, in July 1984, a Brazilian television company Global T.V. – made a documentary about the visit of Exeter City to South America. Exeter City had been the first team to play Brazil in an International fixture. The game was played at the Laranjeiras Stadium in Rio de Janeiro, which was the home ground for the Fluminese Football Club. The television crew visited the home of City's goalkeeper from that tour – Dick Pym – the 91-year-old enthralled the television crew with his memories of the tour for about an hour and a half, relating many stories to them. He did of course point out that, as previously mentioned, he was injured early on in the tour.

The team line-ups in that historic Brazil versus Exeter City meeting on 21st July 1914 were as follows:

BRAZIL: Marcos, Pindaro, Nery, Lagreca, Rubens, Salles, Rolando, Abelardo, Oswaldo, Gomes, Friedenreieh, Osman, Formiga.

EEXETER CITY: Reg Loram, Jack Fort, Sammy Strettle, Jimmy Rigby, Jim Lagan, Fred Marshall, Harry Holt, Fred Whittaker, William Hunter, William Lovett, Fred Goodwin.

The match referee was a Mr Harry Robinson who also played cricket for Brazilian club, Paysandu. Had Dick Pym played, Exeter City might well have beaten Brazil, but had to settle for a 3-3 draw!

Dick told the T.V crew that he had brought a parrot back to England with him, and it survived quite happily at St James's Park for a few years. On the bird's death it was decided to bury it behind the goal at the St James's Road end of the ground. After a short while it was pointed out that since the bird had been buried City had not won a game! So, with footballers being superstitious, the poor parrot was unceremoniously dug up again and buried elsewhere. Legend has it that City's playing fortunes changed immediately for the better.

On leaving Mr Pym, Global T.V. visited St James's Park to film the ground, although the club seemed strangely apathetic towards them. They also filmed in the city centre before returning to their London offices.

Dick Pym died in September 1988, aged 95. He was a marvellous man and, as a mark of respect, Exeter City held a minutes silence before the start of their next home game a few days later against Torquay United.

Another item to be brought back from the tour was the football used in the Racing Club Buenos Aires versus Exeter City match. This again was looked after by Dick Pym, for seventy one years! In June 1985 the ball was offered to Topsham Youth Club for auction to raise funds. The then Exeter City chairman Byron Snell decided that the ball was part of the club's history, and so bought it for £100, donating the cash to the Youth Club.

TRAINING GROUND

The present Exeter City training ground at the Cat and Fiddle is the envy

This photograph is part of a crowd scene at a match from yesteryear. It must have been a nerve-wracking game as the supporter on the far right is smoking two cigarettes at the same time!!

EXETER. V. ARGYLE. 1916.

Games between Devon's league teams have always been keenly contested and usually well supported. The picture on the left shows the two captains of Exeter City and Torquay United before the local derby at St James's Park on 28th January 1933. Exeter won the game 5-0!

(Below) Striker Alan Beer slots a goal in for City in an Easter encounter with Torquay at Plainmoor.

of many Football League clubs. The site is rented to the club by the wife of the club president. But it was back in 1964 that the City first actively sought such a site. The club announced that they were looking for a fifteen acre area as near as possible to the City centre which they could purchase and develop for practice pitches and training facilities.

The City chairman, Reg Rose had been looking for such a site for some time, and in March 1964 it was decided to advertise for the land required. Mr Rose said extra training facilities were badly needed as they could not always use St James's Park when the pitch was unfit. He also envisaged the City Colts side playing their Exeter and District League matches at the new site. The building of an indoor gymnasium was another possibility.

Exeter City first expressed an interest in the Cat and Fiddle site in April 1978. The grounds, which consisted of four football pitches and two rugby pitches, were owned by St Luke's College. The College however merged with Exeter University in the summer of 1978, and Exeter were keen to rent the site. They were fortunate to do so, renting the area from the president's wife Mrs Hill, the training ground proving a great asset and being one of the best in the entire Football League.

TRANSFERS

Exeter City's star inside forward, Harold 'Happy' Houghton was transferred to Norwich City in March 1934, only to make his debut three days later in his new club colours against his old team-mates in a Third Division South League fixture! The result was 1-1, and Houghton didn't manage to score.

One of the oddest transfers involving an Exeter City player was surely that of winger Billy Owen's move to Newport County in May 1937. Owen had joined the City midway through the 1936/37 season after playing for Manchester United and Reading. He scored an outstanding goal against Newport at St James's Park in a 3-1 Exeter win, and it was this which prompted the Welsh club's interest in him.

Owen took a train from Exeter to Newport, met the County manager Louis Page, agreed terms, and within ten minutes jumped on another train back to Exeter! Ironically, Owen made his Newport debut against Exeter at the start of the following season. He retired from playing in 1946, and lived near to Newport County's Somerton Park ground until his death in April 1981.

Exeter City's 18-year-old Honiton-born half back Maurice Setters was transferred to West Bromwich Albion for a fee of £3,000 in February 1955. The directors explained it was a financial necessity, for with mounting costs the club needed attendances of 11,000 to remain on an even keel, and they were only getting around 7,000 to matches at St James's Park.

Here are some of the many players who can claim the distinction of having represented more than one of Devon's three league teams. (Top left) Nicky Jennings played as a winger for Plymouth Argyle before joining Exeter City. (Above) Bobby Saxton not only played for both Argyle and City, but also was manager of both clubs. John Delve (below) is seen here at Pat Wakeham's Testimonial Match against Watford which took place on Monday, 29th November 1982. A major part of John Delve's football league career saw him playing in the West Country for Argyle, City and then Hereford United. He rejoined City until, on ending his league career, he went to play for Elmore in the Western League.

TRAVEL

Exeter City introduced a scheme in March 1989 whereby up to six supporters could travel to away fixtures on the team coach, and stay at the same hotels as the players. The first time the scheme was put into operation was for the match at York City – the cost to include all meals was a mere £85. The idea was to offset the overall cost of travelling to away fixtures which on average totalled £700 per game.

UNITED APPROACH

Exeter City's Board of Directors were represented by Norman Kendall, Sidney Thomas, and Ernest Head, at a meeting described as – 'being both well attended and enthusiastic' – to discuss the possible formation of a Limited Company – Torquay United Football Club – in March 1921. The meeting held in the local Y.M.C.A. was told that talks had been held to merge Babbacombe and Torquay Town Football Club, joint tenants of Plainmoor, to form a new club to be called Torquay United.

Norman Kendall, a director of Exeter City, told the meeting that his fellow directors welcomed the move and the possibility of Torquay United joining the Western League. Exeter City would give their wholehearted support and become shareholders if the new company was formed. He went on to relate the struggle that Exeter had in their early days, and urged the people of Torquay to give financial assistance to the United club.

A vote of thanks was recorded to the Exeter City directors for attending the meeting and for their support. It was reported that £500 was collected after the meeting towards the formation of a Torquay United club.

VICTORY

Before the kick-off at the Exeter City versus Royal Marine Light Infantry match on Saturday 21st October 1905, the Reverend Philip Williams led the cheers of the crowd raised in respect of the memory of Lord Nelson who was mortally wounded at Cape Trafalgar exactly 100 years ago to the day.

The Exeter City directors and team travelled to Portsmouth in September 1921 for a Third Division South fixture. The day before the game the party, which included players Joe Graham and Jim Watson, who were to make their debuts, visited Lord Nelson's old flagship, HMS *Victory* in the Portsmouth Dockyard. The team stayed overnight at the Sussex Hotel in Portsmouth. The game ended in a 2-0 defeat for City in front of l2,000 spectators.

WALKING

A fifteen mile sponsored walk for club funds was organised by the Exeter City Supporters Club in May 1969. Nearly 200 people took part including manager John Newman and several of his players. The oldest walker was 67-year-old Mrs G. Hoare who had been a supporter of the City since 1912. Three girls who took part had to make the seven mile trek from their Dunsford homes before going on to complete the fifteen mile course. Around £500 was raised from the event.

A similar fund raising exercise took place twelve months later when 130 supporters walked around a one and a half mile circuit in the City centre. Again between £500 and £600 was raised, with some of the money going towards the purchase of a set of tracksuits for the City players. The man who covered the greatest distance over the circuit was Exeter City player Steve Morris, who walked and ran twenty nine miles.

WATER BOTTLES

During the 1961/62 season Exeter played three matches at St James's Park against touring sides, O.F.K. Belgrade (Yugoslavia), Offenbach Kickers (West Germany), and C.A.R. La Paz (Bolivia). The South American side were not too happy with a cold night when they visited Exeter, and one of their players went down injured requiring treatment. Spectators were amazed to see not only the La Paz trainer race onto the field, but also another of the party carrying a hot water bottle! He gave this to the injured player to keep him warm whilst treatment was administered. City went on to defeat La Paz 3-1.

WEMBLEY STADIUM

Exeter City have never played at Wembley Stadium, although they now have better chance to do so than ever before with the recent introduction of the end of season play-offs, and the Autoglass Trophy competition. The club have, however, seen their flag fly proudly at the famous old stadium. In March 1967 the Exeter City flag was on view for the Football League Cup Final between Queen's Park Rangers and West Bromwich Albion. The Football League had asked for the last thirty two clubs who were left in the competition and City were among them, to send their official club flag to be flown on Final afternoon.

WHIPPET

Trainer Jimmy Gallagher had a novel idea to improve the speed of the Exeter City players. He occasionally brought his pet whippet along to St James's Park for training sessions! He would give City players a few yards start before letting go of his whippet to try and overtake the player over a set distance! Gallagher was trainer at Exeter between 1939 and 1949.

X-RATED

Exeter City supporters can no doubt recall a few X-rated performances by their red and white shirted heroes. But perhaps the greatest humiliation for any Football League club is to be on the receiving end of a giant-killing act in the FA Cup. Exeter have unfortunately experienced quite a few of these disappointments.

Each season photo-calls are organised as a major publicity event. It is an opportunity to show off the new team strip for home/away games and an opportunity for the manager, in this case Alan Ball, to parade his entire staff for the press.

The squad which started the 1991/92 season

Non-League clubs who have disposed of the City since the Second World War are: Hereford United (1953/54), Bath City (1957/58), Dartford (1961/62), Gravesend and Northfleet (1962/63), Bedford Town (1965/66), Walton and Hersham (1972/73), Alvechurch (1973/74), Maidstone United (1978/79 and 1983/84), Enfield (1984/85), and Bognor Regis Town (1988/89).

YEOFORD TO YORK

No fewer than five teams beginning with the letter 'Y' have been met by Exeter City. The only Football League side, however, is York City.

The other four are, Yeoford and North Tawton League XI, Yeovil Town (formerly known as Yeovil and Petters United), Yeovil Aircraft Works, and Yiewsley (later to be called Hillingdon Borough).

Yeovil were one of City's opponents for a number of years in Southern League and Western League fixtures. Yiewsley were also members of the Southern League in seasons 1958/59 and 1959/60. The Yeoford and North Tawton League were played in a friendly in 1922, and likewise, the Yeovil Aircraft Works also provided friendly opposition in 1919.

ZIDER

A large contingent of younger supporters first began to congregate under the Cowshed during the late 1960s and early 1970s. They formed an unofficial 'Exeter City choir' which could be heard singing various renditions in support of the team. A favourite song of theirs which was heard at all games was a version of – 'Drink Up Thee Zider' – not always in tune either! The Wurzels, whose song it was, made a far better job of it.